I0817504

Dwelling with Dignity

ENACTING CATHOLIC SOCIAL TRADITION

Dwelling with Dignity

Catholic Social Teaching and Homelessness

Suzanne Mulligan

LITURGICAL PRESS
Collegeville, Minnesota
litpress.org

Cover design by Rosemary Strohm. Cross illustration courtesy of Getty Images.

Excerpt from Brendan Kennelly, *Familiar Strangers: New & Selected Poems, 1960–2004* (Bloodaxe Books, 2004), bloodaxebooks.com. Used with permission.

Library of Congress Cataloging-in-Publication Data

Names: Mulligan, Suzanne, author.
Title: Dwelling with dignity : Catholic social teaching and homelessness / Suzanne Mulligan.
Description: Collegeville, Minnesota : Liturgical Press, [2025] | Series: Enacting Catholic social tradition | Includes bibliographical references. | Summary: "In Dwelling with Dignity, Suzanne Mulligan examines how Catholic social teaching can help us to rethink homelessness. It invites us to construct economies and societies that place the human person, and their flourishing, at their center, and to work towards personal and communal healing through accompaniment, solidarity, and a commitment to justice in the world"— Provided by publisher.
Identifiers: LCCN 2024041667 (print) | LCCN 2024041668 (ebook) | ISBN 9780814669853 (trade paperback) | ISBN 9780814669860 (epub) | ISBN 9780814689271 (pdf)
Subjects: LCSH: Christianity and justice—Catholic Church. | Christian sociology. | Homelessness. | Homeless persons.
Classification: LCC BX1795.J87 M85 2025 (print) | LCC BX1795.J87 (ebook) | DDC 261.8/32592—dc23/eng/20241115
LC record available at https://lccn.loc.gov/2024041667
LC ebook record available at https://lccn.loc.gov/2024041668

Contents

Introduction

In 2022 I spent almost five months in the United States enjoying a sabbatical from my university in Ireland. During that time, I visited the University of Notre Dame in Indiana for one week, having been invited by the then–acting executive director of the Center for Social Concerns, Bill Purcell. One evening Bill and I visited a homeless project in South Bend where his university colleague Professor Margaret Pfeil worked. While there, we attended Mass in a small, simple upper room in the shelter. The significance of the location of the *upper* room was not of course lost on me. There was little decoration in this chapel—no ornately painted ceilings or priceless works of art. We sat on folding chairs and knelt on the floor. It was an important space for people experiencing homelessness in the South Bend area; somewhere they could go to quietly reflect, pray, and gather their thoughts. Whereas the downstairs facilities tended to the material needs of people, this upper room provided an opportunity for spiritual nourishment. Only a few of us were there that evening, and I was the visitor, the stranger in the room. I was also a privileged white woman who was educated, enjoyed income security, and had a home. I knew nothing about homelessness, not in any real, personal sense. I have never faced the prospect of being homeless, have never slept rough on the streets, and I do not know what it is like to move around from shelter to shelter. And yet, in that upper room that evening, I felt at peace for the first time in many months. And I felt welcomed.

The contradictions in our world were vividly on display that evening too. While we sat and prayed, the world outside continued as normal. Notre Dame, of course, is a wealthy, prestigious university with world-class facilities. Many of its students come from affluent backgrounds; all of its graduates belong to a small and fortunate group who today receive advanced degrees and are likely to have more opportunities in life because of that. And so it is with our world; incredible wealth resting alongside dire poverty, sometimes only meters apart.

I am conscious as I set out on the journey of writing this book that I cannot tell the full story of homelessness. For that to be heard we must go out onto the streets; listen to the hopes, sorrows, fears, loves, and joys of our unhoused brothers and sisters; and allow ourselves to be transformed.[1] Nor do I write as an expert in economics, politics, social science, or psychology—disciplines that speak to specific dimensions of homelessness in concrete, practical ways. I write as a Catholic theologian, and the aim of this book is to consider how Catholic social doctrine can constructively shape discussion concerning the phenomenon of homelessness.

Catholic social doctrine is a rich body of teaching, covering a range of social issues, and consisting of a library of documents that has been in the making for over a century now. Popes have responded to what we call "the signs of the times," addressing urgent global concerns and bringing the Gospel to bear on world affairs. At this point, it is important to avert to the distinction between the church's social mission and its social doctrine.

The social mission of the Church extends back to the infancy of the Christian faith itself. Christ's mandate to his disciples was to go out into the world and transform it for the better. The Christian faith, in other words, was to be a public faith, always

[1] Some of these stories can be found in Susan J. Dunlap, *Shelter Theology: The Religious Lives of People without Homes* (Minneapolis: Fortress Press, 2021), chap. 4.

journeying to the peripheries and always seeking out the most vulnerable. Our identity as Christians in the world is bound up with a commitment to justice, for love of God and love of neighbor are inseparable. As the *Compendium of the Social Doctrine of the Church* states:

> The Church's social doctrine is an integral part of her evangelizing ministry. Nothing that concerns the community of men and women—situations and problems regarding justice, freedom, development, relations between peoples, peace—is foreign to evangelization, and evangelization would be incomplete if it did not take into account the mutual demands continually made by the Gospel and by the concrete, personal and social life of man.[2]

Paragraph 546 of the *Compendium* reminds us that we do not live two parallel lives—one spiritual and the other secular. Rather, the integration of faith and life is an indispensable part of Christian living. Moreover, in the 1971 synodal document "Justice in the World," this relationship is described as follows:

> Our relationship to our neighbor is bound up with our relationship to God; our response to the love of God, saving us through Christ, is shown to be effective in his love and service of people. Christian love of neighbor and justice cannot be separated. For love implies an absolute demand for justice, namely a recognition of the dignity and rights of one's neighbor. Justice attains its inner fullness only in love.[3]

The 1971 synod also recognized that social action must accompany the teaching and preaching of the church—faith and action go hand in hand: "For unless the Christian message of love and

[2] Pontifical Council for Justice and Peace, *Compendium of the Social Doctrine of the Church* (Washington, DC: USCCB Publishing, 2005) 66.

[3] World Synod of Catholic Bishops, "Justice in the World" 34, Vatican (1971), https://www.cctwincities.org/wp-content/uploads/2015/10/Justicia-in-Mundo.pdf.

justice shows its effectiveness through action in the cause of justice in the world, it will only with difficulty gain credibility with the people of our times" ("Justice in the World" 35).

There have been many times throughout history where the church has fallen short of what God expects. Yet, its social mission has always been an integral part of its identity. In times of crisis—war, famine, or plague—people have turned to the church for sanctuary. And it is its social mission that has inspired the establishment of organizations like St. Vincent de Paul and religious orders dedicated to helping the poor.

The social *doctrine* of the church (more commonly referred to as Catholic Social Teaching or CST) is a more recent development. The term refers to an official body of teaching that has been formulated over the past 130 years or so, comprising encyclicals, apostolic exhortations, conciliar documents, regional bishops' conferences statements, and synodal documents. Beginning with Pope Leo XIII's encyclical letter *Rerum Novarum*, there has evolved a corpus of teaching that addresses urgent social concerns. This teaching continues to expand as church leaders engage with the signs of their own times, applying Christian theology to complex contemporary issues. One also speaks of Catholic social *thought*, referring to a broader category of work that includes the scholarship of theologians and philosophers who investigate, decipher, and critique official CST.

What makes CST different from, say, social science or political science is its account of the transcendent dimension of the human being. Christians believe that all persons are made in the image of God and that our home, our final end, lies ultimately in communion with God. As Anna Rowlands puts it, "The fundamental theo-dramatic construct of CST lies in a vision of social communion, gifted to us, fractured by us and continually in a process of restoration in which we are active, graced, fragile, failing and resilient participants in time."[4] Catholic Social Teaching

[4] Anna Rowlands, *Towards a Politics of Communion: Catholic Social Teaching in Dark Times* (London: T&T Clark, 2021), 6.

promotes a way of living that is founded on principles such as human dignity, justice, solidarity, and a preferential option for the poor. It recognizes the transcendent dimension of human existence and the human search for ultimate truth and meaning. It challenges worldviews that deny the transcendent significance of existence and worldviews that aggressively promote rugged individualism, consumerism, and relativism. The person and her rights are understood in a relational way, and her journeying toward God is recognized as an essential component of what it means to be human.

It is against this background that I reflect upon the complex reality of homelessness. Chapter 1 begins by examining some of the "drivers" of this crisis. In this chapter, I highlight the experience of some groups that are susceptible to homelessness and outline some of the underlying social, economic, and cultural factors that contribute to their precarity. Neither the listing of groups nor causes is exhaustive—such would be impossible within the confines of a chapter. Rather, I wish to focus on certain groups that I believe are either overlooked in some of the scholarship or which assist the aim of the chapter, which is to reaffirm the need for intersectional, sophisticated responses that reflect the multi-layered needs of local communities.

Nor do I situate this opening chapter, or indeed the book, in any one location. The Irish context is the one with which I am most familiar, and the Irish Catholic Bishops' Conference produced an excellent pastoral letter in 2018 in response to Ireland's housing crisis. For this reason, the Irish context is referenced at times throughout the book, albeit that this is not a book about the Irish housing crisis. The book tries to reflect the global parameters of this question, which is why I refer to a number of different locations in the first chapter. But the unique features of homelessness in every locality across the world would obviously be impossible to map here, and chapter 1 attempts the far more modest task of simply introducing the reader to some features of what is a truly global problem.

Chapters 2, 3, and 4 move more directly into the social teaching of the church itself. Some might argue that these chapters could be arranged in a different order. And perhaps they could. However, the areas of CST covered in these three middle chapters are interconnected and are best understood in relation to each other. Chapter 2 examines the concept of the common good. I begin with the common good because it sets out a conceptual framework for later chapters. Human dignity (chapter 3) and integral human development (chapter 4) provide further conceptual apparatus that help critique the homeless crisis. I have taken my cue from the *Compendium of the Social Doctrine of the Church*, which describes the principles of Catholic Social Teaching as reciprocal, complementary, and interrelated. It elaborates: "The principles of the Church's social doctrine must be appreciated in their unity, interrelatedness and articulation. . . . Examining each of these principles individually must not lead to using them only in part or in an erroneous manner, which would be the case if they were to be invoked in a disjointed and unconnected way with respect to each of the others" (n. 162). My hope is that these chapters provide a helpful analysis of these core principles and demonstrates their applicability to debates about homelessness. By focusing on the common good, human dignity, and integral human development, I want not only to consider the material deprivation caused by homelessness but also highlight the spiritual, emotional, and relational damage it entails.

By way of conclusion, chapter 5 asks how the language of accompaniment, hospitality, and vulnerability can be applied to homelessness. My hope is that this may offer an alternative way to think about, approach, and understand the trauma associated with being unhoused.

Anyone interested in homelessness knows that a vast body of scholarship exists on the topic. This book is a very modest contribution to that collection of literature. As I mentioned, I write as a Catholic theologian and as someone who has never been directly impacted by homelessness. I want to acknowledge, therefore, those who work on the front line of homeless ministry, as well as those who are without a home, whose experiences, courage, and resilience inform our understanding and inspire our way forward.

Chapter ONE

The Many Faces of Homelessness

The Gospel tells us constantly to run the risk of a face-to-face encounter with others, with their physical presence which challenges us, with their pain and their pleas, with their joy which infects us in our close and continuous interaction.

(Pope Francis, *Evangelii Gaudium* 88)

Introduction

Imagine access to housing as a ladder: at the top of this ladder are those who enjoy housing security. There are many rungs on the ladder, each representing something that has enabled a person to access a home. Perhaps they have a decent level of income, are in a safe relationship, have sufficient savings to obtain a mortgage, and so on. But if something goes wrong in life, the rungs on the ladder quickly disappear, and we find ourselves slipping toward homelessness. It does not take a lot for this to happen. Think of situations where someone loses a job, or the landlord decides to sell the property, or a person succumbs to an addiction. Or instances where sickness might force someone to work fewer hours, resulting in less income; where marital breakdown or the loss of a partner can lead to depression; or where global events such as the economic downturn in 2008 or the Covid pandemic in 2020 create unexpected precarity; or when natural disasters make an area no longer habitable. Life can present crises that cause one to slip down the housing ladder quickly and unexpectedly. Some of us have security nets that help halt the slide—our family and friends come to our assistance, or we have savings that see us through the tough times. But not everyone has security nets, and it only takes one area of life to fracture for homelessness to become a reality.

The dominant narrative says that the unhoused somehow deserve their lot. If they had worked harder or were more prudent, if they had made better life choices, or if they were better educated, then they would not end up living on the streets. But this is superficial, and the roots of the problem lie deeper. Human beings are fragile, and life is precarious. Sickness, violence, or economic hardship may be just around the corner, and we should not presume to know all the circumstances of any person's life.

This chapter examines some of the factors that can underlie homelessness. I do not offer a comprehensive analysis of all relevant factors but instead wish to concentrate on certain at-risk groups and the systemic injustices that compound that risk.

Any analysis must recognize that many different global realities affect the problem. Climate change, war, human trafficking, and rising economic inequality exacerbate the housing crisis. In local contexts specific factors emerge that need to be worked out in context-specific ways; examples include the marginalization experienced by Indigenous populations, people with disability, people with mental health illness, war veterans, and low-income workers. While later chapters consider the theological and ethical aspects of homelessness, the purpose of this opening chapter is to simply outline some of the parameters of the crisis.

Homelessness: The Global Reality

Approximately 150 million people around the world are homeless. A further 1.6 billion people are living in inadequate housing.[1] This is a human rights disaster. Homelessness represents an assault on human dignity and threatens the realization of fundamental human rights such as the right to privacy, personal security, freedom of religion, and freedom from degrading treatment. The United Nations (UN) explains the scale of the problem as follows: "Homelessness has emerged as a global human rights violation even in States that have adequate resources to address it. It has, however, been largely insulated from human rights accountability, and rarely been addressed as a human rights violation requiring positive measures by States to prevent and eliminate it."[2] The presence of homelessness in our communities represents a failure by governments to care for the common good and protect the fundamental rights of their citizens. State responses have been poor. Even in wealthier countries governments are falling short, partly due to the fact that more governments are handing over the responsibility for the provision of housing to the markets, with disastrous consequences. Some argue that property is a commodity like any other, and that the markets ought to dictate the price of, and access to, this commodity. However, as the UN explains, "only few States have laws that allow people in situation of homelessness to claim access to housing that is adequate, affordable and ensures privacy, beyond regulations governing access to collective emergency shelters. Similarly only few courts have so far taken the courage to oblige public authorities to take all reasonable steps to eliminate homelessness, based on national, constitutional or international human rights obligations."[3]

[1] Ruff Institute of Global Homelessness, "About Us," https://ighomelessness.org/about-us/.

[2] United Nations Special Rapporteur on Housing, "Homelessness and Human Rights," https://www.ohchr.org/en/special-procedures/sr-housing/homelessness-and-human-rights.

[3] UN Special Rapporteur on Housing, "Homelessness and Human Rights."

Importantly, the UN acknowledges that the experience of homelessness includes both lack of housing as well as the absence of any real opportunity of obtaining housing. The UN explains that the experience of homelessness goes far beyond the deprivation of shelter: "Reducing the matter to putting a roof over one's head would fail to take into account the loss of social connection—the feeling of 'belonging nowhere'—and the social exclusion experienced by persons living in homelessness."[4] This is a key point to which I shall be returning. I believe that the dominant discourse about housing and the role it plays in our lives needs to be rethought, and this requires moving away from a way of thinking deeply rooted in economic arguments. Moreover, I hope to show that the Catholic Social Tradition provides resources that allow for a richer understanding of the issue, and help foster a deeper, more human conversation about the right to a home. The alternative is to allow prevailing thinking to continue, where housing is reduced to a commodity, entirely at the mercy of the markets. The Catholic Social Tradition rejects such an approach, as later chapters will demonstrate.

The causes of homelessness are many, and viewed in global terms, displacement from war and violence remains a leading factor. Figures for 2023 show that approximately 110 million people have been forced to flee their homes owing to persecution, war, violence, and human rights violations. This figure represents the highest level of displacement on record. And according to the UN, of this number, 35.3 million are classified as refugees, 62.5 million are internally displaced, 5.4 million are asylum seekers, and 5.2 million are people in need of international protection.[5]

The majority of refugees in the world today are hosted by poorer nations that already struggle to provide resources for their

[4] UN Special Rapporteur on Housing.

[5] United Nations Refugee Agency, "Refugee Statistics," https://www.unrefugees.org/refugee-facts/statistics/.

citizens. The Horn of Africa and East Africa, as well as the African Great Lakes region, hosted 5 million refugees at the end of 2022, for example, while renewed violence in Sudan in 2023 resulted in 2.6 million people fleeing to neighboring countries. In Central America, significant numbers of people in Venezuela, Guatemala, El Salvador, and Honduras have fled local violence. In Europe, the war in Ukraine has added significantly to the numbers crossing borders and seeking sanctuary, while Turkey continues to be the world's largest refugee-hosting country, home to approximately 3.6 million refugees. In Iraq and Syria, many people have been internally displaced, while others who return home after displacement struggle to secure decent housing in the aftermath of war. In addition, the Rohingya crisis in Myanmar has forced millions to flee to Bangladesh and Malaysia. The majority of Rohingya refugees are women, children, and elderly people who require additional aid, medical care, and personal protection. It is believed that 1.2 million Rohingya refugees have fled their homes since the outbreak of violence in 2017.[6] As conflicts intensify across the world, more people will be forced to flee, adding to existing pressure on housing supply.

Climate change is also leading to displacement, and its impact is overwhelmingly felt by the poorest. But as summer wildfires across the Global North remind us, the changing climate is affecting everyone, even those in wealthy countries. Furthermore, we are witnessing flooding, drought, and wildfire events with greater frequency and intensity. More people will face the prospect of fleeing their homes as these natural disasters become commonplace. Many will never return. The unfolding climate crisis is accelerating the movement of peoples to urban settings, displacing people internally, and adding to numbers seeking to cross borders into other nation states. Millions find themselves living in substandard dwellings or being forced to seek refuge in camps and temporary settlements. Although these individuals are not homeless in the

[6] UN Refugee Agency, "Refugee Statistics."

strictest sense, they endure inadequate living conditions and add strain to local housing needs. Global commitment to eradicate homelessness, therefore, must operate alongside a commitment to climate justice and other human rights agendas. The homeless crisis is not an isolated crisis but must be understood in relation to other complex social, economic, and environmental realities.

People who experience homelessness have poorer health outcomes compared to the rest of the population. The harshness of life on the streets inevitably impacts health and well-being. Homelessness causes thousands of premature deaths every year, with many people dying from exposure to bad weather or as victims of violence. It, therefore, intersects with several other social justice issues such as access to public health, domestic and gender-based violence, substance abuse, racial and gender discrimination, unemployment, urban violence, and internal and cross-border displacement. Moreover, we know that levels of homelessness can change suddenly because of unforeseen events, as recent conflicts in Gaza and Ukraine demonstrate. Efforts to tackle homelessness, therefore, must occur alongside other initiatives that seek to improve people's rights and freedoms.

Thus, there are many causes of homelessness. As I mentioned above, anyone can face the prospect of homelessness if the right conditions exist. The rungs on our metaphorical ladder can easily, and unexpectedly, disappear. To use another analogy, Marybeth Shinn compares the housing crisis to the game "musical chairs":

> In the analogy, the players are poor households, and the chairs are the housing units they can afford; if there are fewer affordable units than poor households, some will be left homeless when the music stops. The children who fail to nab chairs are those who move more slowly than others. Similarly, individuals and families who fail to obtain housing, under conditions of scarcity, are those who are most vulnerable, by reason of individual factors or social exclusion. However, the level of scarcity is a joint function of housing supply,

> prices, and subsidies; incomes at the bottom of the distribution; and social welfare spending.[7]

Thus, the structural causes of homelessness include growing economic inequality, poorly paid and ununionized jobs, few legal protections for renters, and lack of access to adequate healthcare. Other factors include addiction, mental illness, having been in foster care or the prison system, or having experienced gender-based violence. Moreover, oppression on the basis of race, sexual orientation, ethnicity, or disability can heighten housing insecurity.

What Is Homelessness?

Homelessness refers to people living on the streets or in cars, those who are in temporary emergency accommodation such as women's shelters, those who have fled war and violence and are residing in refugee camps, those who are living in severely compromised shelter, and those who are "couch surfing." The United States Department of Housing and Urban Development (HUD) describes homelessness as anyone who is lacking a "fixed, regular, and adequate" nighttime shelter.[8] Rough sleepers, once thought of as the face of homelessness, are no longer the only, or most prevalent, category of unhoused person today. Thus, narrow definitions of homelessness fail to capture the extent of the problem or recognize the many different cohorts who are at risk of slipping into homelessness. Hence, homeless people have come to be classified in a variety of ways, which facilitates a better appreciation of risk and corresponding response. Experts identify transitional

[7] Cited in Laura Stivers, *Disrupting Homelessness: Alternative Christian Approaches* (Minneapolis: Fortress Press, 2011), 33.

[8] HUD Exchange, "Category 1: Literally Homeless," https://www.hudexchange.info/homelessness-assistance/coc-esg-virtual-binders/coc-esg-homeless-eligibility/four-categories/category-1/. See also Matthew Adkins, "Homelessness in America: Statistics, Analysis, and Trends," Security.org, last updated June 7, 2024, https://www.security.org/resources/homeless-statistics/.

homelessness, episodic homelessness, and chronic homelessness,[9] each capturing certain characteristics that inform our understanding. Poverty emerges time and again as the common denominator across most, if not all, groupings.

Transitional homelessness refers to people who find themselves homeless once or twice in their lifetime, usually because of some unexpected crisis like the loss of one's job, divorce, the death of a partner, the loss of a child, mental health problems, and so on. In these moments in life, a person turns to others for help, usually family, friends, or neighbors. This support network provides a temporary place to stay. In other instances, an individual may stay in hotels for a period of time. In such cases, being homeless does not become a permanent feature of a person's life and this individual has sufficient "safety nets" to ride out times of hardship.

Episodic homelessness refers to the situation of people who are in and out of homelessness on a regular basis and for different lengths of time. This would include people who are in jail, in detox clinics, in hospitals, and who slip back into homelessness after spending some time off the streets. Homelessness is a relatively regular feature of this person's life but is interrupted by time away from the streets too.

Chronic homelessness, by contrast, refers to people who spend most of their lives living on the streets or in homeless shelters. These people usually have great difficulty finding jobs and permanent shelter, and perhaps cannot access the healthcare services or

[9] Taken from Stivers, *Disrupting Homelessness.* However, various homeless organizations use slightly different terms, including "hidden homelessness," which refers to people who are homeless but not captured in national or local homeless statistics because they are staying with relatives, friends, and so on. See Comic Relief, "What Are the Four Types of Homelessness?," December 6, 2021, https://www.comicrelief.org/posts/what-are-the-four-types-of-homelessness, for further information. Or see HUD, "Children and Youth and HUD's Homeless Definition," https://files.hudexchange.info/resources/documents/HUDs-Homeless-Definition-as-it-Relates-to-Children-and-Youth.pdf, where homelessness is categorized as "literal homelessness," "imminent risk of homelessness," "homeless under other statutes," and "fleeing domestic violence."

social security supports they need to reintegrate into society and secure stable housing.[10]

Homeless organizations identify gender, race, ethnicity, and age as risk factors contributing to housing insecurity.[11] The single largest homeless demographic in the United States is men, and among single men, veterans emerge as an at-risk group—military veterans make up 20 percent of unhoused people in the United States (we return to this below). The majority of homeless families—the population of homeless people with children—are headed by women. In terms of racial and ethnic patterns, African Americans and European Americans make up most homeless people in the United States. Interestingly, Laura Stivers notes that one-fourth of the urban homeless population in America is employed.[12] And we see similar trends in Ireland too, as more and more single- and double-income families are becoming homeless due to rising rents and a housing market that is beyond the reach of lower-income individuals. Among the many faces of homelessness, therefore, are families, workers, children, veterans, and elderly people.

Elevated Risk: Some Key Groups

Any effort at understanding homelessness must begin on the streets. For here we find the many faces of homelessness: people who are displaced and forgotten, the migrant, the veteran, women and children, the abused, the religiously and culturally ostracized, the exiled. We must see their faces and hear their stories because these encounters bring us face to face with the hypocrisy of our world. Our socioeconomic structures have created systems of exclusion, and it is why Pope Francis calls for

[10] Stivers, *Disrupting Homelessness*, 31.

[11] See Adkins, "Homelessness in America," https://www.security.org/resources/homeless-statistics/, for further analysis of homeless statistics in the United States.

[12] Stivers, *Disrupting Homelessness*, 32.

authentic encounter between people. He believes that we can no longer remain "indifferent to suffering; we cannot allow anyone to go through life as an outcast. Instead, we should feel indignant, challenged to emerge from our comfortable isolation and to be changed by contact with human suffering" (*Fratelli Tutti* 68). We must go to the streets, become a "field hospital" for the poor, and we must commit ourselves to building up communities based on "a universal love that promotes all persons" (*Fratelli Tutti* 106). In this section I wish to consider some specific groups vulnerable to homelessness, focusing on women, military veterans, young people, and LGBTQI+ people. I have chosen these groups because they are often underrepresented in homelessness debates, but also because their elevated vulnerability illustrates the connection between homelessness and social, cultural, and economic marginalization.

Women and Homelessness

In global terms, women do not enjoy the same political, economic, and social freedoms as men. And in times of crisis, that lack of freedom places them at additional risk. Whether we speak of displacement due to climate change, of being forced to flee war and conflict, or of the burdens imposed by poverty, women are exposed to precarity in ways that can push them into homelessness.

Typically, women across the world lack the same economic empowerment as men and have fewer assets; they are less educated and often do not enjoy the same degree of food security as their male counterparts. Race plays its part here too—poorer women of color are at greater risk of poverty, homelessness, and sexual and physical abuse than white women. Moreover, efforts to alleviate homelessness must cater to the needs of women who have children or who are pregnant. And women who have experienced physical or sexual abuse might require access to the specific services that can provide the emotional and psychological help they need.

Writing about the violence faced by unhoused women in India, Julie George says that women's vulnerability is owed in part to unjust female stereotypes. Although domestic violence is one of the leading causes of homelessness among women, gender stereotypes and lack of economic freedom forces many to remain in their abusive settings. Citing Elisabeth Schüssler Fiorenza, George explains the extent of the problem:

> The cult of true womanhood proclaims that the vocation of women is housemaker. The fulfillment of her true nature and happiness consists in creating the home as a peaceful island in the sea of alienated society, [an] Eden-Paradise to which men can retreat from the exploitations and temptations of the work-world. Women must provide in the home a climate of peace and happiness, of self-sacrificing love and self-effacing gentility in order to save the family.[13]

What George calls the "cult of domesticity" reinforces the low status of women in India. And although women's place is believed to be in the home, they rarely have control over that property or the family income. The home, therefore, has become the battleground for women: it is the place where they encounter violence, while cultural norms and economic destitution make it very difficult for women to leave. Citing Judy Tobler, Erin Brigham also raises the problem of the home as a place of violence for women. The home is not always a sanctuary for women—it can be the place where physical violence and sexual assault are routine.[14]

For the women who do leave, or those who are evicted from their home by their partner, the streets pose enormous risk. Cities are violent places for women and girls—rape, kidnapping, sexual

[13] Julie George, SSpS, "Violence, Violations, and Homeless Women," in *Street Homelessness and Catholic Theological Ethics*, ed. James F. Keenan SJ and Mark McGreevy (New York: Orbis Books, 2019), 44.

[14] Erin Brigham, *Church as Field Hospital: Toward an Ecclesiology of Sanctuary* (Collegeville, MN: Liturgical Press, 2022), 168.

exploitation, and murder are common. George explains that in India most shelters offer accommodation to women and children for only a very short time, and consequently provide little hope of medium-term housing security and escape from the streets.

George also explains the practice of "witch-hunting" in India, which she describes as one of the worst forms of cultural violence done to women.[15] Within this patriarchal society, scapegoating of women or their branding as witches often goes culturally unchallenged. Widowed, single, divorced, or deserted women are especially vulnerable to homelessness, and it is not uncommon for people with vested interests to accuse them of witchcraft in the hope of acquiring the homes or some other property. "Witch-hunts are most common among poor rural communities with little access to education and health services, but with lasting, age-old belief in witch-craft," George explains.[16] She also says that women's lack of control over land and property in India significantly increases their chances of becoming homeless at some point in their lives. Therefore, the empowerment of women must go hand in hand with property rights and legal access to the home. Finally, George explains that old age can be a particularly difficult time for women. Older women are usually dependent on their children for shelter and security and if daughters become homeless, older generations find themselves with little option but to turn to life on the streets.

A woman's right to housing and to land is systematically denied in many parts of the world, and, as George notes, this creates the context in which women's human rights are easily violated: "Women's contributions to family and society remain unrecognized, and mostly unpaid; thus, the need for women to be able to secure land and housing has become critical."[17] And although some countries have implemented greater legal protection for

[15] George, "Violence, Violations, and Homeless Women," 46.

[16] George, 46.

[17] George, 49.

women's housing rights, it often proves ineffective in the face of patriarchal attitudes that continue to oppress women and girls.[18]

I use the Indian example to illustrate the complex nature of homelessness, especially for women living in social and cultural contexts where patriarchy and misogamy go largely unchallenged, and where their socioeconomic and cultural disempowerment enjoys cultural approval. It reminds us that effective solutions must be multilayered and strategic, and that protection of women's human rights is intimately linked to housing security. And what must the church do? Citing Varghese Theckanath, George concludes that

> the most important step forward for the Church in urban India is to trace its roots back to the poor. If it placed its best personnel and resources at the service of the elite in the last century, the same has to be done for the poor today. The Church has to physically, psychologically, and voluntarily move to the periphery of society to protect human rights, create gender parity, and help reduce the impact of climate change.[19]

Anna Perkins writes about homeless women in Jamaica, where we see many problems similar to those described by George. Perkins laments that homelessness has become part of the urban landscape in Jamaica. Although a greater number of males are officially recorded as homeless, females constitute what she calls "disguised" or "hidden" homeless, with little official account taken of homeless women and girls.[20] The point Perkins makes here is important because this hidden dimension of homelessness often evades official statistics. She writes: "Women and children are to be found predominantly among the concealed homeless. Concealed

[18] George, 49.

[19] George, 51.

[20] Anna Perkins, "Moving Again: Women, Catholic Social Teaching, and Disguised Homelessness in Jamaica," in Keenan and McGreevey, *Street Homelessness*, 256.

homelessness occurs when someone loses her home because of a combination of various factors, including displacement due to gang/political violence . . . economic hardships, relationship loss/abandonment, mental illness, HIV/AIDS status, substance abuse, or . . . natural disasters."[21] It is common in these circumstances to find children dispersed across wider family settings, living with aunts, uncles, cousins, or other extended family members. This "dispersal" of children can create additional occasions of neglect and abuse.

Domestic violence is a major cause of homelessness among women and children in Jamaica. Cycles of vulnerability and violence emerge, and Perkins believes that local churches must condemn more forcefully all forms of gender-based violence. She is critical also of the Jamaican government's failure to tackle homelessness, describing it as "one of the worst forms of urban poverty and social vulnerability." She goes on to say that it is a terrible failure of governance and demonstrates the state's lack of commitment to the common good and the welfare of Jamaican citizens.[22]

Although writing from very different contexts, both Perkins and George describe many common risks that elevate women's vulnerability, most notably poverty and gender-based violence. Cultural norms further embed these injustices into the social fabric of each locality. Moreover, policies aimed at reducing homelessness must include the experiences, vulnerabilities, insights, and needs of women. Protecting women's rights, especially their economic, educational, health, and property rights, is critical. As Perkins says, we need to ensure that women are "counted and consulted."[23]

[21] Perkins, "Moving Again," 256.
[22] Perkins, 256.
[23] Perkins, 262.

Veterans

I turn next to veterans and look at why they constitute such a high proportion of homeless people in the United States.[24] American veterans provide an interesting example of how a government, and indeed society, can muster the moral will to respond effectively to homelessness. For although by no means perfect, national efforts to tackle homelessness among veterans has enjoyed some success.

US veterans of recent wars—especially Iraq and Afghanistan—have tended to become homeless more quickly after exiting the military than have the veterans of previous wars. Post-traumatic stress disorder is likely to be a contributing factor, but Thomas Byrne, professor of social work at Boston University, believes that the reality is more complicated and requires deeper analysis. One reason why veterans are a high-risk group, Byrne holds, is that they are no longer representative of the general population. Switching to an all-volunteer force has led to more people from poorer backgrounds joining the military, and this may help explain why more veterans are becoming homeless. People from poorer, less advantaged backgrounds are typically at heightened risk, and if members of this same socioeconomic cohort are joining the military in greater numbers, it seems plausible to suggest that they are at heightened risk of homelessness after exiting armed service.

Approximately thirty-seven thousand veterans are homeless in the United States today, but this number has decreased by about 50 percent since 2009. This is largely thanks to substantial investments in housing by the Department of Veterans Affairs (VA) over the past decade or so. In instances where veterans receive housing assistance, they are more likely to remain stably

[24] For more information on veterans in the United States, see United States Department of Housing and Urban Development, *Veteran Homelessness: A Supplemental Report to the 2009 AHAR to Congress*, https://www.huduser.gov/portal/sites/default/files/pdf/2009AHARVeteransReport.pdf.

housed.[25] But despite these gains, Byrne identifies a more general lack of affordable housing as a leading cause of homelessness among veterans.

There is a lot of stigma around homelessness, but Byrne notes that homeless veterans are less stigmatized because of the high social status they hold. This has led to positive political action on behalf of homeless veterans, with considerable investment in housing and related services for ex-military personnel. While this is certainly welcomed, the same political will and public support for funding other homeless projects does not exist.

Dennis P. Culhane and Ann Elizabeth Montgomery also examine veteran homelessness in the United States, explaining that: "The global scale of veteran homelessness is daunting, as virtually every corner of the world has produced survivors of war whose traumatic experiences and dislocation from home and community have rendered so many excluded from society."[26] Yet, the United States has gone a considerable way toward tackling homelessness among veterans, and Culhane and Montgomery believe that this is due to both evidence-based policies and strong political will. In 2009, Barack Obama set the goal of ending veteran homelessness as part of his presidency. When he became president, Veterans Affairs spent around $300 million on support programs related to health and transitional housing for veterans. By the time Obama left office, that figure had risen to $1.6 billion, and covered many projects including homelessness prevention and the provision of permanent housing for more than 200,000 veterans annually.[27] This increase in funding was due mainly to cross-party political

[25] Thomas Byrne, interview with Andrew Thurston, "Why Veterans Remain at Greater Risk of Homelessness," *The Brink*, November 9, 2022, 8, https://www.bu.edu/articles/2022/why-veterans-remain-at-greater-risk-of-homelessness/.

[26] Dennis P. Culhane and Ann Elizabeth Montgomery, "Homelessness among Military Veterans: The United States as a Recent Case Study in Political Will and Evidence-Based Policymaking," in Keenan and McGreevey, *Street Homelessness*, 64.

[27] Culhane and Montgomery, "Homelessness among Military Veterans," 66.

will, but also reflected the strong moral imperative among wider society that veterans' welfare ought to be a priority. Byrne makes this point too. However, this raises important moral questions about merit and compassion: Do we believe some groups deserve more support than others, and if so, why? Our decision-making is often the result of biases and prejudices that we may not even recognize. James Keenan, SJ, helpfully distinguishes between merited and unmerited suffering, and says that our responses of compassion tend to be directed toward those we believe are enduring unmerited suffering. "If we insist on this distinction," he claims, "a deep residue of moralism is apparent wherever listeners are encouraged to sift out the 'merited' from the 'unmerited' sufferers. . . . The distinction allows us, I think, the opportunity to parse out our sympathy in very condescending and stingy ways."[28] The point Keenan makes here is crucial. No one deserves to be without a home. But as the US response to veteran housing demonstrates, we regularly decide who merits our compassion and who does not owing to unjust stereotypes and biases or because of the high social standing attributed to certain groups.

The success of the VA in the United States tells us that political will and practical solutions can be found. But as I mentioned, success here is connected to the high moral status of veterans in US society, raising interesting questions about merit that need to be acknowledged.

Another reason for the success of the VA is the evidence-based approach that they employ. This is seen through the VA's universal screening for housing insecurity, the work of the Support Services for Veteran Families initiative, and a rental subsidy scheme to ensure that housing is affordable and that supportive services are available. All these initiatives combine to help lower the number of veterans who are homeless. Culhane and Montgomery believe that other countries and many nongovernmental organizations

[28] James F. Keenan, SJ, *Moral Wisdom: Lessons and Texts from the Catholic Tradition* (Oxford: Sheed and Ward, 2004), 74–75.

could learn from this approach, and in particular from the successful outcomes of evidence-based programs that incorporate the specific needs of different groups.[29]

A subgroup that warrants special mention is women. Culhane and Montgomery explore why female veterans, many of whom have children, are at particular risk of homelessness. The number of homeless women veterans is on the rise as more females enter the armed forces. Many of these women "double up" with friends and family rather than turning to traditional homeless services, and this makes it difficult to trace them in official records. These women represent another form of the "hidden" homelessness that Perkins mentioned above. Moreover, female veterans will have specific housing needs, especially as they relate to childcare and healthcare. Again, here we see the need to include their voice if strategies are to be effective and targeted.

Finally, Culhane and Montgomery highlight the aging profile of veterans. As they get older, their housing needs will change. This is true of aging populations generally, but veterans may have specific physical and psychological needs that change with time. More assisted living accommodation that caters to their unique needs will be required, especially for older servicemen and -women with physical disabilities and mental health concerns.

What is interesting about Byrne's research, as well as that of Culhane and Montgomery, is that it reveals the success of veteran housing initiatives. Much more needs to be done, of course, and military personnel remain a high-risk group in America. But we see what can be achieved when political will and strategic, evidence-based initiatives combine.

[29] Culhane and Montgomery, "Homelessness among Military Veterans," 68.

Young People and LGBTQI+ Homelessness

It is difficult to find accurate figures for the number of young people who are homeless today.[30] The transient nature of youth homelessness makes it hard to get a real sense of the scale of this problem, and many young people go undetected by census-gathering initiatives. In Ireland, however, we know that many families are becoming homeless because of a housing crisis, with inevitable consequences for children. Of the 13,532 people accessing emergency accommodation in Ireland in the first months of 2024, approximately 4,027 of them were children. A further 5,617 young people under the age of twenty-four living in emergency accommodation.[31] In addition, 2,000 families are relying on temporary, emergency accommodation in Ireland at present.[32]

Turning to the American context, Alejandro Crosthwaite outlines the risks faced by young people on the streets: they are less likely to receive a stable education or have access to adequate healthcare and psychological services, for example. They are vulnerable to physical, psychological, and sexual abuse, and are more likely to engage in high-risk survival activities such as prostitution. Infection with STDs such as HIV is a real prospect for many young people living on the streets. They are also prone to depression, substance abuse, poor nutritional practices, low self-esteem, and untimely death. Every year in the US, approximately five thousand homeless young people

[30] Unless otherwise stated, I use the term "young people" to include both children and young adults. A child is defined as anyone under the age of eighteen years, and a young adult is anyone between eighteen and twenty-four years.

[31] See The Peter McVerry Trust for these figures, available at www.homelessnessireland.ie.

[32] See Shauna Bowers and Jack Horgan-Jones, "Homeless Figures Hit New Record with More Than 4,000 Children in Emergency Accommodation," *Irish Times*, January 5, 2024, https://www.irishtimes.com/ireland/social-affairs/2024/01/05/number-of-people-in-emergency-accommodation-hits-new-high-of-13514/.

die because of physical and/or sexual assault, avoidable illness, or suicide.[33]

Crosthwaite believes that understanding the root causes of youth homelessness will lead to earlier and more effective interventions. Poverty is a leading reason why young people become homeless. It elevates vulnerability and is one of the systemic causes of global homelessness. In fact, poverty is arguably the most visible common denominator across all groups of homeless people. Crosthwaite explains that "in many situations, as the youth got older, their families were unable to continue to support them financially, and thus they were forced to leave their homes—not because they were being kicked out, but because their family's poverty meant they could no longer continue living with them."[34]

Another cause of youth homelessness is some form of family dysfunction, whether that be parental neglect, substance abuse within the home, family violence, or sexual abuse within the family. Thirty-two percent of young people who are homeless report a high degree of family chaos as a contributing factor.[35] For others, being in juvenile detention facilities elevates risk. Crosthwaite explains that African American children under the age of five become homeless at twice the rate of their white counterparts: "Similarly, racism and discrimination continue to keep unemployment rates high among African Americans, consequently increasing their risk for homelessness. Mass incarceration of people of color, particularly African American men and boys, further increases their likelihood of becoming homeless."[36]

He goes on to explain that homophobia too can push some young people into homelessness. Rather shockingly, of the 1.6 million homeless young people in the United States, almost 40 percent identify as LGBTQI+, even though the LGBTQI+ community

[33] See Alejandro Crosthwaite, OP, "Youth and LGBT: Homeless, Overlooked, and Undeserved," in Keenan and McGreevey, *Street Homelessness*.

[34] Crosthwaite, "Youth and LGBT," 80.

[35] Crosthwaite, 80.

[36] Crosthwaite, 82.

only represents 7 percent of the population.[37] Many believe religion encourages negative, toxic, attitudes toward homosexual and transgender people. Family rejection plays its part too, especially where strong religious or cultural beliefs about gay people shape attitudes within the home. "Those LGBT youth who left because of sexual orientation identity conflict and internalized homophobia were at greater risk of suicidal thoughts," Crosthwaite explains.[38] The degree of trauma suffered by LGBTQI+ young people on the streets is poignantly captured by Crosthwaite when he cites Carl Sicilano, director of one of the largest shelters for LGBTQI+ people in the United States. It is worth quoting the passage in full, for it perfectly and provocatively explains the nature of the problem. Sicilano is writing an open letter to the *New York Times* in advance of the 2015 Synod on the Family. Sicilano is asking Pope Francis to support young LGBTQI+ homeless people and to recognize their suffering, trauma, and marginalization.

> I ask you to take urgent action to protect them from the devastating consequences of religious rejection, which is the most common reason LGBT youths are driven from their homes. . . . What these youths endure is horrific. They endure the torment of being unloved and unwanted by their parents, combined with the ordeals of hunger, cold and sexual exploitation while homeless. LGBT youths who are rejected by their families are 8 times more likely to attempt suicide than LGBT youths whose parents accept them. . . . A teaching's wisdom and efficacy must be judged in part by its outcome. The teaching that homosexual conduct is a sin has a poisonous outcome, bearing fruit in many Christian parents who abandon their LGBT children to homelessness and destitution.[39]

An important step forward, therefore, must be the provision of safe spaces and different forms of ministry that respond to the

[37] Crosthwaite, 82.
[38] Crosthwaite, 83.
[39] Cited in Crosthwaite, 84.

trauma experienced by these young people. This will include investment in faith-based and non-faith-based shelters for youths, the provision of family reconciliation services, transitional housing for young people, psychological services, and safe spaces for them to speak about their suffering, neglect, and abuse. Later in this book I shall argue that street ministries play a crucial role in helping people to rebuild their lives. In chapter 4 I will explore how the spiritual accompaniment of homeless people is an essential element of integral human development. But it is clear from Crosthwaite's account that significant time and resources must be invested in the spiritual healing of young people on the streets. Ironically, church teaching is part of the reason why LGBTQI+ youths are becoming homeless and why they feel so unloved, unwanted, and traumatized by their faith communities. And yet church-based street ministries find themselves at the heart of the homeless crisis and have an opportunity to respond to the deep human needs of young people whose lives have been fractured by homelessness. Erin Brigham, speaking about the work done by the Gubbio Project in San Francisco, says that women and LGBTQI+ people living on the streets experience Gubbio as doubly redemptive—it is both a church and a home space in which they can find rest and surety.[40] God's love is not exclusive, and by reaching out to LGBTQI+ young people with compassion, mercy, and gentleness, we do God's work in the world.

Conclusion

The purpose of this introductory chapter is to illustrate some dimensions of the homelessness crisis. By considering different geopolitical locations, as well as different high-risk groups, we can see how vulnerability and homelessness are connected. It cannot be a comprehensive treatment, but I hope it has shown the complexity of the issue and the need for intersectional, sophisticated

[40] Brigham, *Church as Field Hospital*, 168.

thinking when discussing homelessness. The following three chapters apply principles of Catholic Social Teaching to this topic; I argue that the church's social teaching provides a conceptual framework and language that can enrich debates about homelessness, critique its root causes, and imagine future possibilities.

Chapter TWO

The Common Good and Social Participation

> *Home! . . . Now, with a rush of old memories, how clearly it stood up before him, in the darkness! Shabby indeed, and small and poorly furnished, and yet his, the home he had made for himself, the home he had been so happy to get back to after his day's work. And the home had been happy with him, too, evidently, and was missing him, and wanted him back . . .*
>
> (Kenneth Grahame, *The Wind in the Willows*)

Introduction

In chapter 1 I highlighted some groups at elevated risk of homelessness, adverting to social, economic, and cultural factors that underlie their predicament. This chapter explores the concept of the common good, as it is used in Catholic Social Teaching, with attention given also to the related principles of participation, contributive justice, and subsidiarity. These concepts are especially relevant to a constructive engagement with the problem of homelessness, given its complexity.

One of the effects of homelessness is that it reduces opportunities to contribute fully to society. The common good is a complex idea, but its realization depends in part on active, responsible citizens who are willing to contribute to society and commit themselves to a shared idea of a common life enjoyed together. Homelessness makes this less achievable because it denies people the chance to reside in a place long enough to integrate fully and forge an identity. But equally, the common good consists of the social conditions that enable people to reach their fulfillment. Thus, it concerns those structures, policies, laws, and processes that enhance human rights and freedoms. It reveals an understanding of society that is dynamic, inclusive, and dignity focused.

Socioeconomic inequality undermines the common good in a myriad of ways. As societies become more unequal, the common good becomes harder to realize. Inequality deepens social divisions, and when economic policies prioritize the freedom of the markets and disproportionately benefit the few, this has devastating consequences for the equitable provision of social goods such as housing. The failure of current economic structures are becoming evident to even some of the wealthiest individuals. For example, on September 7, 2023, a letter appeared in the *Irish Times* calling for new taxes on the rich. Among the signatories were several Irish politicians and MEPs, economists Thomas Piketty and Joseph Stiglitz, US senator Bernie Sanders, Abigail Disney, music composer Brian Eno, politicians, millionaires, and businesspeople from as far away as Hong Kong and Australia, and representatives of organizations such as Millionaires for Humanity, Patriotic Millionaires, and Earth 4 All. They explained: "The accumulation of extreme wealth by the world's richest individuals has become an economic, ecological and human rights disaster, threatening political stability in countries all over the world. Such steep levels of inequality undermine the strength of virtually every one of our global systems and must be addressed." Their proposal is to "make our international and national systems work for everyone, not merely those who have money and power. With this in mind, we call on the members of the G20 to work together to enact new tax regimes—at national and international levels—that eliminate the ability of the ultra-rich to avoid paying their dues and introduce new rules that determine higher taxation of extreme wealth."[1]

The same criticism of this concentration of wealth is found in Catholic Social Teaching. Building on his predecessors' theology, Pope Francis warns of the dangers of rising inequality and the abuses of neoliberalism. The neoliberal might argue that as wealth grows, so too does its distribution. Trickle-down economics is based on the belief that as overall wealth increases, a larger portion of it eventually finds its way to the poor. However, the evidence is that inequality is worsening. Theologian Gerald Beyer explains that although worker productivity has increased since the 1940s, the median wage for males in America is less than it was thirty years ago, adjusting for inflation. For females, the situation is worse. Women in America earn seventy-seven cents for every dollar that their male counterparts earn, and so their median wage is even lower in real terms. The average CEO in the United States today earns three hundred times what the average worker earns. And Beyer adds that American families work five hundred more hours than they did in 1979, with implications for family life and childcare.[2]

Pope John Paul II described neoliberalism as follows: it is a system "based on a purely economic conception of [the human person;] this system considers profit and the law of the market as its only parameters, to the detriment of the dignity of and the respect due to individuals and peoples. At times this system has become

[1] "The True Cost of Extreme Wealth—a Letter to the Editor by Economists, Artists and Politicians Calls for New Taxes on the Rich," *Irish Times*, September 7, 2023, https://www.irishtimes.com/opinion/letters/2023/09/07/the-true-cost-of-extreme-wealth-a-letter-to-the-editor-by-economists-artists-and-politicians-including-bernie-sanders-thomas-piketty-and-brian-eno/.

[2] Gerald J. Beyer, "Strange Bedfellows: Religious Liberty and Neoliberalism," *National Catholic Reporter*, February 15, 2012, https://www.ncronline.org/news/politics/strange-bedfellows-religious-liberty-and-neoliberalism.

the ideological justification for certain attitudes and behaviour in the social and political spheres leading to the neglect of the weaker members of society. Indeed, the poor are becoming ever more numerous, victims of specific policies and structures which are often unjust" (*Ecclesia in America* 56). Neoliberals argue that this economic ideology has heralded greater freedom—freedom of the markets, freedom of enterprise, freedom from the shackles of state, and so on. But in truth, neoliberalism has succeeded only in increasing inequality across the world, in strengthening the power of global systems and organizations, in exploiting labor and weakening workers' rights, and in justifying the plundering of the earth's resources for short-term economic benefit. It has increased the number of tax havens for the ultra-rich and has exacerbated what Pope Francis calls a "throw-away culture."

Proposing a New Way of Thinking

Neoliberalism has dire consequences for the provision of housing, as explained by Steven Bouma-Prediger and Brian J. Walsh in their book *Beyond Homelessness: Christian Faith in a Culture of Displacement*. They argue that the root causes of homelessness lie with inequitable social and economic policies. Homelessness is not the result of laziness or unintelligence, or because some people have less moral character than others. "Rather, it is 'simply the end point of the "logical" outcome for part of the population—the extremely poor—under conditions of industrial and urban decay.' Indeed, anyone who has lived among the homeless would acknowledge that they 'are not deficient and defective; they are resilient and resourceful.'"[3] Bouma-Prediger and Walsh insist that what is at fault is the economy itself and the way it is structured. They are critical of public policy and a cultural

[3] Steven Bouma-Prediger and Brian J. Walsh, *Beyond Homelessness: Christian Faith in a Culture of Displacement* (Grand Rapids, MI: Eerdmans, 2023 edition), 93.

mindset that prioritizes economic growth above all else. Pope Francis too warns of the dangers of this mindset when he says, "Today everything comes under the laws of competition and the survival of the fittest, where the powerful feed upon the powerless. As a consequence, masses of people find themselves excluded and marginalized: without work, without possibilities, without any means of escape" (*Evangelii Gaudium* 53). Bouma-Prediger and Walsh reject trickle-down economics, saying, rather provocatively, that in this system of oppression, what trickles down is the blood of the poor.[4]

The problem is not just that "trickle-down" economics is failing the poor but that economies are structured in such a way that the poor are increasingly considered unimportant. The poor are also excluded from the "new economy" which is an economy built for highly skilled individuals who have advanced degrees, usually in technology, engineering, finance, and science. For those trying to survive on minimum wage, barely able to make ends meet and possibly working two or three jobs, access to housing remains problematic. The jobs of the "new economy" are not the jobs that the working poor can access, who are often just one paycheck or one illness away from not being able to pay their rent. Think back to the image of a ladder in chapter 1—losing your job or missing one shift at work might be all it takes for the rungs of the ladder to disappear, causing a slide toward homelessness.

Bouma-Prediger and Walsh place the blame for the housing crisis firmly within this context. Neoliberalism and globalization have created economic structures that make access to housing and other basic needs more challenging for the poor. But more than that, neoliberalism and globalization have created a *culture* that legitimizes this exclusion, and as Pope Francis says, deadens us to the suffering of those around us. I agree with Bouma-Prediger and Walsh when they say that we cannot properly address homelessness and poverty until we acknowledge the damaging effects

[4] Bouma-Prediger and Walsh, *Beyond Homelessness*, 95.

of globalization.[5] What is needed is a radical change of structures as well as a cultural shift and change of attitude.

Writing as they are from the US and Canadian contexts, Bouma-Prediger and Walsh identify several reasons for the homeless crisis. One is the lack of affordable housing. This is also true of the Irish context where spending on social housing was cut by 72 percent between 2008 and 2012, falling from 1.38 billion euros to 390 million euros. The Irish government is now trying to address this shortfall in social housing but is playing catch-up with high demand. We also know that the construction of private homes in Ireland fell dramatically during those years. Similarly, in Toronto no new social housing units were built between 1996 to 2000. Spending on affordable housing fell from $1.1 billion in 1994 to zero by the end of 1998. And in in the United States, when Ronald Reagan became president in 1981, the federal government spent seven dollars on defense for every one spent on housing. By the time Reagan left office in 1989, the ratio had jumped to forty-six to one.[6] These statistics reveal the huge deficit in spending on social and affordable housing, but, importantly, social policies also reveal social values. Policies tell us what is important at a given moment, and for America under the Reagan administration the priority was not the provision of safe, affordable housing for lower-paid workers.

Another factor identified by Bouma-Prediger and Walsh is the lack of social safety nets for people. Neoliberals might argue that the state has no business interfering in the provision of housing. The market, left to its own devices, will produce housing, determine its value based on supply and demand, and create employment that will lift people out of poverty.[7] This approach removes responsibility for the provision of affordable housing from the state and places it solely on the markets. Bouma-Prediger and

[5] Bouma-Prediger and Walsh, 97.
[6] Bouma-Prediger and Walsh, 99.
[7] Bouma-Prediger and Walsh, 102.

Walsh argue, "The abandonment of housing by national governments has given the private market ample opportunity in the last twenty years to develop housing for the poor. The results have been devastating."[8] It results in a lack of housing for the poor, but it also creates a system that gives ultimate authority to the markets. And it is an ideology that insists that government should not create social safety nets for people.[9] These concerns were also voiced by the Irish Catholic Bishops' Conference, writing in 2018: "Homelessness and poor housing conditions are, to a large degree, the result of past and current political and economic choices . . . we must be clear that the deepening housing crisis has been created by a series of choices" ("A Room at the Inn?" 16).[10]

Bouma-Prediger and Walsh reject "trickle-down" economics, insisting that "increased economic growth bears no positive relationship to alleviating poverty or homelessness; indeed, the opposite is the case. Poverty and homelessness rise hand in hand with the global economy: there is no trickling down of wealth."[11] This is echoed throughout the social teaching of the church. The right to property is not an absolute right; it is conditional, and must be exercised responsibly. Moreover, individual rights rest alongside social responsibilities. And so, governments must create the conditions, including economic conditions, in which individual rights can be enjoyed and protected in an inclusive, proportionate way. This is why, in 1977, the Irish Bishops stated that "unless the basic human rights of all are safeguarded through just legislation and just structures then the very process that makes some people richer will result in making others relatively or even absolutely poorer. . . . The Christian must keep insisting that property, wealth and

[8] Bouma-Prediger and Walsh, 102.

[9] Bouma-Prediger and Walsh, 102.

[10] Irish Catholic Bishops' Conference, "A Room at the Inn? A Pastoral Letter on Housing and Homelessness" (Dublin: Veritas, 2018) 16.

[11] Bouma-Prediger and Walsh, 103.

profits . . . are not absolute rights but carry with them weighty moral and social responsibilities."[12]

Part of the bigger problem is the absence of a collective consciousness when it comes to economic decisions. Are we happy to hand over all decision-making to those in positions of authority, and allow the markets to determine the allocation of housing and other basic needs? Bouma-Prediger and Walsh explain that

> the power of this ideology, the intractable nature of homelessness, and the absence of political or civic will to take steps to address the realities of homelessness all indicate that the crisis before us is not narrowly economic in nature but is a crisis of culture and an erosion of the values that might shape the public good. . . . If there is to be a cultural shift, it must entail a renewed economic paradigm "that proceeds from the assumption that people need to advance the interest of others." . . . In other words, we must abandon the ideological worldview of globalization, with its penchant for privatizing what is public, for absolutizing the impersonal forces of the "market" and for forsaking civic responsibility.[13]

Bouma-Prediger and Walsh use the notion of *habitus* to explain this point further. By *habitus* they mean a *way of being*, a habitual state of living and thinking, a disposition, inclination, or mindset that encourages us to act in a certain way. It refers to the habitual patterns we develop in our thinking and acting that foster certain ways of seeing the world, rooted in what they call "shared dispositions, values, and orientations."[14] But why do some ideas, values, and patterns of behavior form a culture and not others? What is it that shapes our thinking and influences our decision-making? Social habits, they say, are rooted in a shared habitus. So, has apathy or indifference to social injustice become part of our shared

[12] Irish Catholic Bishops' Conference, "The Work of Justice: Pastoral Letter of the Irish Bishops" (Dublin: Veritas, 1977) 19.

[13] Bouma-Prediger and Walsh, 106.

[14] Bouma-Prediger and Walsh, 107.

habitus? Has moral laziness crept in, deepening our indifference to the suffering of others?

The dominant habitus at present, one might argue, legitimizes the exclusion of the poor, discarding them in a "throw-away culture." This justifies the existence of economic and social structures that provide a comfortable standard of living for some, but poverty for others. What Bouma-Prediger and Walsh say here is not dissimilar to Michael Sandel's critique of meritocracy,[15] or to what economist Joseph Stiglitz writes about economic inequality. Stiglitz warns that, "with extreme inequality, the nature of our society changes in fundamental ways. Those at the top come to believe that they are entitled to what they have. And this can lead to behaviours that undermine the cohesiveness of society. Those excluded from prosperity begin to expect the worst from governments and leaders. Trust is eroded, along with civic engagement and a sense of common purpose."[16] What Stiglitz says here is critical. Inequality is having a deep impact across society, seen not only through rising poverty levels but also through a growing disillusionment within society. Solidarity and social trust are being eroded, giving rise to complex social and political issues in our world.[17] We find in Catholic Social Teaching a countercultural message, however, one that might help cultivate a new mindset able to alleviate the social tensions that Stiglitz identifies.

Bouma-Prediger and Walsh also fear that the ideology of neoconservative globalization has become so prevalent in society that displacement of the poor, tax cuts for the rich, and reduced

[15] See Michael Sandel, *The Tyranny of Merit: What's Become of the Common Good?* (London: Allen Lane, 2020).

[16] Joseph Stiglitz, "Inequality in America: A Policy Agenda for a Stronger Future," *Annals of the American Academy of Political and Social Science* 657 (January 2015): 17.

[17] For example, see Anne Applebaum, *Twilight of Democracy: The Failure of Politics and the Parting of Friends* (London: Penguin Books, 2021), for an excellent insight of how inequality and the excesses of globalization are contributing to the rise of populism and far-right groups throughout the world.

spending on social welfare have become accepted as the natural—even the right—thing for governments to do in the interests of economic growth.[18] They call this the habitus of a post-care society. The priority here is to increase wealth and economic growth at any cost. Care comes *post* economic growth, in the sense that it comes after everything else has been secured.[19] The Catholic Social Tradition provides an alternative viewpoint, where the person is placed at the center of decision-making, and where social and political structures are at the service of all persons. Catholic Social Teaching provides a radically different worldview to the sort of "post-care" society that Bouma-Prediger and Walsh describe.

One problem here (and one might identify several problems) is that this way of thinking may seem too shallow. For "the economic growth of the last ten to fifteen years has done little to change the cultural mood regarding responsibility to the poor," Bouma-Prediger and Walsh claim. And it is hard to disagree with them. I recall the rhetoric that dominated public discourse in Ireland around 2008 when, following the collapse of the Irish economy, the public was told that the priority was to stabilize the banks and grow the economy. Everything else could wait, and all other matters would fall into place once the economy was fixed. And yet, despite now having returned to full employment, with ample financial resources at the Irish government's disposal, homelessness continues to rise. Bouma-Prediger and Walsh suggest that this post-care ideology is too shallow to "sustain the kind of renewed civic *habitus* that could creatively and ethically respond to the crisis of homelessness. . . . The culture of fear has given birth to an ethos of individualism, scarcity, survivalism, and withdrawal from social responsibility."[20] Establishing an ethic of care within this cultural mindset will be challenging. But I contend that this is precisely where Catholic Social Teaching becomes

[18] Bouma-Prediger and Walsh, *Beyond Homelessness*, 107.

[19] Bouma-Prediger and Walsh, 107.

[20] Bouma-Prediger and Walsh, 109, 110ff.

crucial, and its message could help form a different habitus of engagement, care, and inclusion.

Bouma-Prediger and Walsh are critical of a habitus of exclusion, reinforced by narratives that tell us the poor are diseased, dirty, violent freeloaders. It excludes because it creates barriers, both physical and attitudinal, that keep the poor seperate. They conclude:

> We need a richer, deeper, and thicker *habitus*, a worldview rooted in a narrative that engenders a culture of hospitality and justice. We need a renewed imagination and renewed cultural practices that can counter a geography of exclusion with an ethos of inclusion. . . . If our personal and cultural imaginations have been captivated by a fearful, self-protective, and myopic ideology of economic growth . . . we need to be set free by a radical narrative of hospitality and homecoming.[21]

The Irish bishops too have called for a change in consciousness regarding housing. They insist that the provision of housing must be understood as part of a wider Christian ethic: "As Christians, our obligation to people who are homeless or poorly housed is unequivocal for it is Christ who is homeless." They go on to say that commitment to those who are homeless is not an "optional extra." Instead, "such a commitment is an inescapable consequence of accepting God's commitment to humanity" ("A Room at the Inn?" 23–24). And they say that the commodification and financialization of housing requires far greater public debate and social analysis. This is part of the wider call within Catholic Social Teaching to develop a new mindset and foster new attitudes toward the marginalized. Pope Francis condemns a "throwaway culture" that now extends even to human beings. Charles Camosy captures the essence of this "throwaway culture" as follows:

> Our . . . culture . . . encourages us to use dehumanizing words and images to describe the poor and the stranger. People with their

[21] Bouma-Prediger and Walsh, 111, 112.

> children fleeing violence are called "illegals." They are "swarms" of "undesirables" and "parasites." [We] must call attention to language that reduces the dignity of marginalized populations to mere catchphrases. Otherwise we objectify the vulnerable and allow ourselves to discard them at will—often at the service of consumerist culture and often in the face of terrible violence.[22]

If Bouma-Prediger and Walsh are correct, and if we need a richer, deeper, and more meaningful habitus, one that promotes a culture of hospitality, inclusion, and justice, can Catholic Social Teaching help achieve this? I believe that it can, and I turn next to the idea of the common good. For this is a concept that provides a counterweight to the individualistic, consumerist ethos of contemporary society. The idea of the common good offers a language and conceptual apparatus that challenges the very problems that Bouma-Prediger, Walsh, and others have outlined and could help generate a new habitus that would make us more attuned to the needs of others.

What Is the Common Good?

The roots of this idea lie in ancient Greek and Roman thought, but it has featured in Christian theology since at least the time of St. Augustine, and it is an important concept in the thinking of St. Thomas. In *Gaudium et Spes* the council fathers describe the common good as "the sum total of social conditions which allow people, either as groups or as individuals, to reach their fulfillment more fully and more easily" (26). And in *Dignitatis Humanae* we read that "the common good of society consists in the sum total of those conditions of social life which enable men to achieve a fuller measure of perfection with greater ease. It consists especially in safeguarding the rights and duties of the human person" (6).

[22] Charles Camosy, *Resisting Throwaway Culture: How a Consistent Life Ethic Can Unite a Fractured People* (New York: New City Press, 2019), 188.

Both descriptions provide a helpful starting point. First, we can say that they are very positive statements; the common good is not limited to the minimal conditions necessary for subsistence but rather points to an understanding of the human person that is vibrant and full of possibility. The common good includes *all* the conditions that facilitate human flourishing, those that afford people opportunities for fulfillment and in which humans can find meaning and lead lives that are considered valuable.

The human person is a relational animal; our lives are enriched by the positive human relationships that envelop us. We think first of our intimate relationships, our family ties, or perhaps our close friendships, and how these connections deepen our existence and give it purpose. But we belong to a much broader social community also. We rely on others whom we may never meet, and we have responsibilities to the collective that need to be honored. Living in right relationship within a community, where rights sometimes clash and where tough decisions about the just distribution of society's benefits and burdens need to be made, is a tricky business. This is the realm of the common good.

This social aspect was captured by the late Pope Benedict in his encyclical *Caritas in Veritate*: "Besides the good of the individual, there is a good that is linked to living in society: the common good. It is the good of 'all of us,' made up of individuals, families and intermediate groups who together constitute society. It is a good that is sought not for its own sake, but for the people who belong to the social community and who can only really and effectively pursue their good within it . . . " (7). But, of course, as society becomes more pluralist, and as people compete for limited resources, achieving the common good can be difficult, even fraught. There are two challenges, therefore, that one might identify at this stage: One is practical and concerns how best to distribute social benefits and burdens given that resources are not limitless. The second is in the intellectual order; how do we determine what the common good is? And, perhaps more importantly, *who* determines what it is?

Constructing the Common Good

In Latin the word *construo* means "to construct." But it also means "to identify." This is helpful, for in order to construct something (a building, for example) one must first identify what is being constructed. Buildings need to be designed, and only then should their physical construction begin. And so it is with the common good. We must imagine its requirements, its shape, and its parameters before we start to construct (build) our vision.

It is precisely here that difficult questions arise: Who determines what the common good is, or what the "sum total of conditions" necessary for human flourishing look like? Should governments decide the requirements of the common good, or are they charged only with its protection? And do we trust governments to protect the common good? As Lisa Cahill notes, globalization has changed our ideas of authority and sovereignty. She explains that "the age of globalization has also displaced the idealized view of authority as consisting precisely in an office of care for the common good and replaced it with a realistic reading of authority as power propelled by self-interest. This has caused a lack of trust in national officials, elected or not, to work for the common good."[23] As social trust continues to erode, and as we witness the influence of fake news on social and political trends, suspicion of government institutions deepens. What Cahill identifies here will continue to have a profound impact on our collective ability to converse about, and generate the will to implement, the requirements of the common good.

Populist and far-right groups are benefiting from a growing sense of political disillusionment. Fake news, conspiracy theories, misinformation, and disinformation create an image of a political elite who either do not care for the average person or do not

[23] Lisa Sowle Cahill, "Globalization and the Common Good," in *Globalization and Catholic Social Thought: Present Crisis, Future Hope*, ed. John A. Coleman and William F. Ryan (New York: Orbis Books, 2005), 44.

understand their struggles. And as Michael Sandel believes, the challenge before us is not only to "imagine a politics that takes moral and spiritual questions seriously, but brings them to bear on broad economic and civic concerns, not only on sex and abortion." He goes on to say that the common good must be founded on citizenship, sacrifice, and service. A just society depends on solidarity and a strong, resilient sense of community. For this to happen, we must find ways to cultivate within people an awareness of, and concern for, the collective. In short, we must "find a way to lean against purely privatized notions of the good life, and cultivate civic virtue."[24] The challenge articulated by Sandel is made difficult by the impoverishment of public discourse and by political agendas that appear more interested in sowing division rather than bringing communities together. It is for this reason that Pope Francis calls for a politics of the common good in *Fratelli Tutti*. The common good presents a horizon of meaning that is rich and inclusive, one that respects the complexity, uniqueness, and giftedness of the human being while also acknowledging the strains and stresses that can exist between people. In this worldview, difference is seen as a gift and not a threat.

Nevertheless, tensions arise, and the common good demands that we make tough decisions in complicated situations. But what we find in Christian theology is an overwhelmingly positive, even confident understanding of the common good. It is rooted in a Christian anthropological approach that recognizes the inherent dignity of all people, their relational calling, and a picture of human happiness that has both earthly and transcendent dimensions.

The Good of Human Relationships

The first characteristic I wish to identify is the good of human relationships. In *Caritas in Veritate*, Pope Benedict says that

[24] Michael Sandel, *Justice: What's the Right Thing to Do?* (New York: Farrar, Straus and Giroux, 2009), 262, 263–64.

one of the deepest forms of poverty that any person can experience is isolation. "If we look closely at other kinds of poverty, including material forms, we see that they are born from isolation, from not being loved or from difficulties in being able to love. Poverty is often produced by a rejection of God's love, by man's basic and tragic tendency to close in on himself, thinking himself to be self-sufficient . . ." (53). Benedict understood that this relational starting point is difficult to achieve today. He argued that societal change would require "a *deeper critical evaluation of the category of relation*" (53, emphasis added). Benedict was hoping for the richer, thicker habitus of which Bouma-Prediger and Walsh write. He understood the importance of positive human relationship for wider human well-being: "As a spiritual being, the human creature is defined through interpersonal relations. The more authentically he or she lives these relations, the more his or her own personal identity matures. It is not by isolation that man establishes his worth, but by placing himself in relation with others and with God. Hence these relations take on fundamental importance" (*Caritatis in Veritate* 53).

Thus, the Christian vision of the common good is a highly relational one. Contrary to a rugged individualism, the social underpinnings of the common good suggest that the good of any person is connected to the good of others. Indeed, our well-being is measured in the context of the flourishing (or not) of those around us. And so, we say that true meaning in life is found not in external commodities or material things but in the fostering of authentic, life-enhancing relationships, including our relationship with God. Of course, if people are to live dignified lives, they need access to various commodities and services, such as adequate health and educational services, or opportunities to achieve a just income. But thinking of the common good in terms of general welfare (which is heavily utilitarian in approach), public interest, or indeed public goods is flawed because of the extrinsic focus of each.[25] For this reason, theologian David Hollenbach explains that positive relationships are in fact the "preconditions" for the sharing of goods and commodities within society. And these relationships are as much a part of the common good as the physical, material items we utilize. He explains that "the quality of such relationships among a society's members is itself part of the good that is, or is not, achieved in it. One of the key elements in the common good of a community or society, therefore, is the good of being a community or society at all. This shared good is immanent within the relationships that bring this community or society into being."[26] Thus, nurturing positive social relationships is a common good. As Hollenbach says, a shared life of communication, ideas, and interactions ought to be valued for its own sake.

Within this context, social bonds and collective identities are forged, and meaningful relationships are enjoyed. It is the context out of which civic virtue emerges too. In other words, there is a good, Hollenbach insists, in being a community at all.[27] Of course, what Hollenbach describes is made easier in situations where people can enjoy a measure of stability and security. And access to housing certainly helps forge the kind of connections mentioned by Hollenbach here. This is not to say that common bonds of mutuality cannot exist among homeless people, but the broader common goods outlined by Hollenbach are attainable more easily with access to secure housing.

Establishing healthy social relationships within our communities presupposes a degree of mutual respect and recognition. This makes genuine social interaction possible, and social interaction is the foundation of a vibrant society. Hollenbach explains that mutual respect enhances the good of all, and that this respect is

[25] See David Hollenbach, *The Common Good and Christian Ethics* (Cambridge: Cambridge University Press, 2002), 7–8.

[26] Hollenbach, *Common Good and Christian Ethics*, 8–9.

[27] Hollenbach, 81–82.

therefore a shared or common good. "It is a good that is realized when the members of society share in creating their life together. This good is truly common when all members of society jointly create a common life together."[28] This highly relational aspect of the common good has been emphasized throughout the Christian tradition and helps balance excessively individualistic approaches to social ethics. It recognizes that, although a shared life together can be fraught at times, and although it depends on sacrifice and compromise, there is a collective good in being able to live together in ways that respect the other in all her uniqueness and difference.

Care and the Common Good

Scholars like David Hollenbach and Patrick Riordan have identified the importance of care for the common good. Hollenbach believes that care and solidarity are among its most valuable dimensions. In the absence of solidarity, a community risks fragmenting and falls short of what it might otherwise achieve.[29] Riordan examines how positive relationships strengthen the common good and forge deeper solidarity among peoples. Our relationships shape our identities as individuals, and the communities to which we belong play a crucial role in forming moral character, discerning the values and virtues worth protecting, and developing the capacity among people for critical evaluation and moral choice. Communities are also where the virtue of care is nurtured, or not. A community's willingness to participate in the difficult discourse around collective meaning and common purpose requires willingness on the part of individuals. We sometimes call this buy-in: people need to buy-in to the common project, knowing that they will be required to make sacrifices and compromises for the common good. And through this buying-in and participation "individuals

[28] Hollenbach, 70–71.
[29] Hollenbach, 189.

engage in communal activity and subject themselves to the standards of a tradition."[30]

As we have seen, Bouma-Prediger and Walsh argue that the current emphasis on the free market and economic growth has created "post-care" societies. Riordan believes that an ethic of care could help reorient common good discourse. He identifies the virtue of care as itself an important feature of the common good, and although the language of care is often absent from public debate, one can see why Riordan places such value on it. "A primary quality of human relationship is care. Most of the work of caring-for in the cultures familiar to us is done by women. The reflection on social order produced by men tends to downplay the importance and value of care, and so the language available for talking about the public domain tends to reflect the elements familiar from typical male experience."[31] It should not seem strange to place care at the heart of our social agenda; we are reliant on others, and we need the care of others to sustain us in times of difficulty. In chapter 5 I examine the idea of vulnerability, and consider how scholars like Linda Hogan apply this idea to international politics. She has argued that an ethic of vulnerability could help reorient the current political landscape. Thus, the language of care and vulnerability is featuring more in contemporary debates about the nature and scope of the common good.

There is a balance to be struck here, of course. On the one hand, an ethic of care could help address an overly individualistic ethos in society. However, the value of autonomy is an important value, especially for women whose identity might otherwise be restricted to caring roles in the home. Undoubtedly, an ethic of care could enrich public discourse. But virtues can be manipulated to advance unjust ends, and Riordan rightly suggests that an ethic of care requires serious investigation and prudent application. For

[30] Patrick Riordan, *A Grammar of the Common Good: Speaking of Globalization* (London: Continuum, 2008), 154.

[31] Riordan, *Grammar of the Common Good*, 162.

example, we saw in chapter 1 how Julie George warned about the "cult of domesticity" and how it is used to limit women's agency by keeping them in the home. Kochurani Abraham, also speaking from the Indian context, expresses similar concerns. In India, cultural norms prioritize "feminine virtues" such as submission, self-sacrifice, and passivity, while social narratives reinforce the idea that preservation of the family is primarily a woman's responsibility. These gender stereotypes heighten female vulnerability since they make it difficult, even dangerous, for women to speak out for fear of family breakup. The cost of this to women is seen in many ways. For some, their agency is diminished. For others, they face helplessness amid increasing vulnerability to violence within home, Abraham says.[32] Erin Brigham expresses similar concerns. She writes, "Associating the domestic sphere with essentialist notions of women as nurturing and self-sacrificing reinforces a gendered social order. . . . The resulting cultural romanticization of the home has not only excluded women from the public sphere, but it has also rendered domestic concerns as private or dangerously invisible."[33] What both Kochurani and Brigham say is very important, and confirms Riordan's hesitation about any universal, unscrutinized promotion of the virtue of care.

However, I agree with Riordan that we need to develop further an ethic of care as part of the common good, and I think this would go some way to dealing with the problems of "post-care" societies that Bouma-Prediger and Walsh highlight. Such an ethic would need to be approached prudently. And our understanding of social virtue requires careful analysis so as not to inadvertently create a new set of social problems. Ultimately, Riordan believes that an ethic of care points to "the importance of attending to the quality of nurturance and formation which is provided to young

[32] Kochurani Abraham, "Resistance: A Liberative Key in Feminist Ethics," in *Feminist Catholic Theological Ethics: Conversations in the World Church*, ed. Linda Hogan and A. E. Orobator (New York: Orbis Books, 2014), 99.

[33] Brigham, *Church as Field Hospital*, 167.

members of society and its future citizens, since they in their turn will condition what will be possible in social and political order."[34]

Dialogue, Listening, and the Common Good

A third characteristic of the common good is dialogue. Current public discourse, often dominated by individualistic and consumerist rhetoric, is creating a cultural mindset unconducive to a common good framework with its focus on obligation, duty, and civic responsibility. Riordan puts it in the following terms, echoing Bouma-Prediger and Walsh's earlier arguments: "The poverty of the rights rhetoric means that the dominant model assumed in the debates is that of individuals who relate to a state without intermediary institutions or communities. As a result, it is difficult to speak about these communities in which young people acquire the *habits of participation* in deliberation, service of others and commitment to values."[35] A feature of this problem, identified also by Michael Sandel, is the impoverished character of public discourse. Sandel believes that a renewed engagement with the idea of the common good would enrich debates about society and our shared lives. Rather than avoid tough questions, we must engage with them. The alternative is to ignore those with whom we differ, but avoidance makes for what he calls a "spurious respect" and inadequate public discourse.[36]

Therefore, our understanding of the common good must include the search for meaning, and mutual respect is one precondition of this search. Discovering shared meaning requires inclusive, respectful, and sustained dialogue, including respectful dialogue with "the stranger." For without this we risk becoming closed off, insular, and suspicious of difference. What Hollenbach calls "intellectual solidarity" plays a vital part in this search for meaning. It describes an orientation or instinct toward intellectual

[34] Riordan, *Grammar of the Common Good*, 163.

[35] Riordan, 155–56, emphasis added.

[36] Sandel, *Justice*, 268.

engagement across religious and cultural boundaries, where difference is seen positively and not something to be feared. The idea of intellectual solidarity welcomes alternative ideas about the good to help shape one's worldview, not in a naive way but in a spirit of sympathetic yet critical inquiry. Hollenbach believes that intellectual solidarity is crucial if we are to revitalize the idea of the common good and find new, imaginative ways forward in creating just, inclusive societies.[37]

The diverse nature of many communities calls for intellectual solidarity, for we otherwise risk becoming ideologically entrenched, extreme in our views, and seeing others as nothing more than rivals to the things we desire. Diversity is not an insurmountable obstacle to a shared vision of the good life, and the dialogue that ensues from engagement with other traditions is itself a good to be encouraged. And in response to those who claim that the intellectual solidarity is either unattainable or is a delusion, Hollenbach confidently states:

> To declare that such intellectual solidarity is unattainable would be to maintain that the idea of the common good is a utopian fantasy . . . Such an outcome would be both a betrayal of the Christian tradition and treason to the possibilities human intelligence can discover. Both Christian faith and the reasonable hopes of humanity lead us to expect more.[38]

Participation, Contribution, and Subsidiarity: Key Features of the Common Good

Participation and Contribution

Three related principles that deepen our understanding of the common good deserve attention at this point. They are the

[37] Hollenbach, *Common Good and Christian Ethics*, 138.
[38] Hollenbach, 158.

principles of participation, contributive justice, and subsidiarity. The common good encompasses both rights and responsibilities. Therefore, it is not something we are given per se but something we must work at and try to establish—it is something achieved *within* communities and *among* communities, and is something that requires ongoing, sustained effort. Citizens contribute to the common good in practical ways by paying taxes, abiding by just laws, and so on. But we contribute in other ways too. As we saw above, intellectual encounter is important, for it allows us to work out together the demands of the common good. Or, to put it differently, Sandel says that "[a] just society cannot be achieved simply by maximizing utility or by securing freedom of choice. To achieve a just society we have to reason together about the meaning of the good life, and to create a public culture hospitable to the disagreements that will inevitably arise."[39]

The principle of participation is founded on the belief that human agency is itself a good, and that it is an integral part of human dignity. The *Compendium of the Social Doctrine of the Church* describes the principle of participation as a "series of activities by means of which the citizen contributes to the cultural, economic, political and social life of the civil community to which [she] belongs" (189). The *Compendium* goes on to explain that participation is a cornerstone of "all democratic orders and one of the major guarantees of the permanence of the democratic system" (190). Participation captures the inherently social nature of the person, and her right to have a say over the direction of her life. It is important for the common good too, for society flourishes when its citizens are informed, engaged, and active. Participation can be witnessed in several ways, but we usually think of political and economic freedoms. For this reason, civil society organizations, structures and institutions that give people a greater voice in society, and which foster moral agency have a crucial role to play here. One might think of the role that trade unions play in

[39] Sandel, *Justice*, 261.

protecting the rights of workers, or of other civic bodies, voluntary or professional, that encourage participation in our communities.

Civil society organizations encourage healthy public discourse and provide spaces for people to discuss, discern, and debate the meaning of the common good. These organizations provide the spaces and opportunities for people to cultivate the "habits of participation" that Riordan mentions, and can perhaps help cultivate the new kind of habitus that Bouma-Prediger and Walsh call for. Civil society helps instill the habits and practices that are so crucial for the common good. Moreover, civil society organizations provide information and help keep governmental institutions accountable.

Thus, civil society has an important role to play in today's globalized world. Local and midrange groups can help shape governmental policy in the process. Yet, any reform from below presupposes active participation in the quest for the common good. Cahill writes:

> The notion of the common good has always begun from the experienced needs and good of human beings, and from insights into the sorts of social relationships that promote human welfare. It has always included subcategories like mutual accountability, subsidiarity, and participation. Thus it provides for social action and responsibility at the local level and anticipates collaboration toward broader structural patterns and lines of authority. And it has always envisioned the interpretation of the human and societal common good with Christian virtues of charity and solidarity, providing for the engagement of religious communities and churches with the common good on the many levels at which the common good itself is actualized.[40]

In their 1986 pastoral letter "Economic Justice for All," the United States bishops' conference spoke of the correlation between inclusive societies and social participation. They explained that social justice implies an obligation on all people to be "active and

[40] Cahill, "Globalization and the Common Good," 44.

productive participants in the life of society and that society has a duty to enable them to participate in this way" (71).[41] They condemned the social structures that perpetuate inequality, deepen disadvantage, and inhibit certain groups from contributing to society because of their race, ethnicity, or economic status. These sinful structures diminish a person's ability to contribute to society, potentially undermining civic virtue and eroding a shared sense of solidarity and the common good. Thus, contributive justice is a feature of integral human development and of the common good, for we each have an obligation to contribute to society, and we must be afforded the *opportunity* to contribute to society. Contributive justice is dependent upon just social structures that encourage people to make positive social contributions.

Contributive justice can be described as "doing justice by guaranteeing those opportunities for integral human development, which so many people are lacking."[42] As far back as 1971, the Synod of Bishops drew attention to the relationship between contributive justice and poverty. They stated that "the influence of the new industrial and technological order favors the concentration of wealth, power and decision-making in the hands of a small public or private controlling group. Economic injustice and lack of social participation keep people from attaining their basic human and civil rights" ("Justice in the World" 7–8). They also noted how growing inequality leads to, what Kate Ward describes as, "hyper-agency" among the wealthy.[43] In brief, hyper-agency describes how those with access to wealth have a greater say over political

[41] United States Conference of Catholic Bishops, "Economic Justice for All: Pastoral Letter on Catholic Social Teaching and the U.S. Economy" (1986), https://www.usccb.org/upload/economic_justice_for_all.pdf.

[42] Tebaldo Vinciguerra, "Contributive Justice and Ecology: A Contribution After the Encyclicals *Laudato si'* and *Fratelli tutti*," *Journal of Catholic Social Thought* 18, no. 2 (2021): 272.

[43] Kate Ward, *Wealth, Virtue, and Moral Luck: Christian Ethics in an Age of Inequality* (Washington, DC: Georgetown University Press, 2021); see chap. 5 in particular.

and social mechanisms, often using this agency to further their own economic interests. The less well off, and especially the poor, have a lesser say over the political and financial structures, and are therefore less likely to effect change. It becomes a cycle whereby the poor have less say over their lives, resulting in growing resentment across large sections of society who feel forgotten and irrelevant.

Inequality, and the hyperagency it fuels, contradicts the very essence of the common good. As the council fathers reminded us in *Gaudium et Spes*, "The best way to fulfill one's obligations of justice and love is to contribute to the common good according to one's means and the needs of others" (30). This suggests that we each have something to contribute to society, and that through our civic participation we strengthen democratic institutions. Furthermore, contributing to society affords us a sense of belonging and helps shape our identity. Contributive justice must be understood inclusively, therefore—it is something that all ought to enjoy.

Paul Gomberg identifies four pillars upon which true contributive justice must be based.[44] First, he rejects meritocracy, since a meritocratic approach legitimizes inequality and the hyperagency of the rich.

A second pillar of contributive justice is what Gomberg calls "good governance." Gomberg insists that contributive justice must include substantive social and participatory democratic structures that seek to protect the rights of all citizens.

Third, there must be commitment on the part of citizens themselves to go beyond what is minimally required by law. There is need for honest, robust examination of the values and ethos of society, and it requires buy-in from citizens. If we seek societies that are more just, compassionate, and inclusive, then we must consider the kind of contribution citizens can make to the common good. And as stated above, people must have the opportunity to make these contributions.

[44] Paul Gomberg, *How to Make Opportunity Equal: Race and Contributive Justice* (Oxford: Blackwell, 2007), chap. 13.

Finally, Gomberg explains that contributive justice and subsidiarity are linked. It is vital that local groups have the means to become involved in decision-making. Evidence shows that the empowerment of communities is crucial in tackling complex issues such as climate change, for example. The utilization of local expertise is a valuable resource as well as an important dimension of contributive justice in action. I return to this point below when I discuss the connection between subsidiarity and responses to homelessness.

There are other ways we can see contributive justice at work. Mark Banks, for example, explores how contributive justice and cultural work are connected. He explains that "contributive justice is concerned with ensuring that everyone has an equal opportunity *to make some kind of social contribution.* It derives from the Aristotelian notion that what we *do* in life is as important as what we *get* in terms of our overall quality of life and well-being. Thus, while distributive justice emphasizes what we might receive or get from society, contributive justice emphasizes what opportunity we might have to *give* to society, in pursuit of different personal or social priorities or goals."[45] Similarly, Cristian Timmermann outlines the social implications of contributive justice: the first is to recognize that people have an *obligation* to contribute to society. But for this to happen, people must have the *opportunity* to contribute to society. Second, contributive justice depends on social structures that facilitate or enable people to make that positive contribution. This includes erradicating structures that fuel discrimination based on gender, race, ethnicity, religion, and so on.[46] Timmermann condemns what the Catholic moral tradition calls the "sinful structures" that perpetuate social inequalities and inhibit certain groups from contributing fully to society.

[45] Mark Banks, "Cultural Work and Contributive Justice," *Journal of Cultural Economy* 16, no. 1 (2023): 51.

[46] Cristian Timmermann, "Contributive Justice: An Exploration of a Wider Provision of Meaningful Work," *Social Justice Research* (2018): 31, 85–111.

Subsidiarity, the Common Good, and Homelessness

I turn finally to the concept of subsidiarity. The principle of subsidiarity assumes the right to associate, and affirms the belief that nothing should be done by a higher authority that cannot be done by a lower one. The *Compendium of the Social Doctrine of the Church* explains that subsidiarity "protects people from abuses by higher-level authority and calls on the same authorities to help individuals and intermediate groups to fulfil their duties. This principle is imperative because every person, family and intermediate group has something original to offer to the community" (187). William Cavanaugh applies this principle to homelessness, arguing that the state, through its promotion of property rights, is in fact a leading contributor to the crisis.[47] By prioritizing private ownership of property over its social nature, Cavanaugh says the state contributes to homelessness in the following ways:

- promoting zoning laws that discourage social and affordable housing, homeless shelters, and other facilities for homeless people in order to protect the market value of properties in certain locations
- enforcing laws that protect the absolute right to property, irrespective of whether it is being used or not—for example, implementing stronger eviction laws for people squatting on disused land
- enacting laws and policies that encourage the gentrification of areas, putting the price of property beyond the reach of local populations
- enacting laws and policies that encourage property and land speculation
- criminalizing homelessness

[47] William T. Cavanaugh, "Strategies from Below: Subsidiarity and Homelessness," in Keenan and McGreevey, *Street Homelessness*, 148.

- enacting laws that encourage the removal of homeless people from semipublic spaces such as shopping malls, restaurants, and fast-food establishments
- enacting laws and policies that connect education funding to property taxes, resulting in better schools in wealthier areas[48]

Like Sandel and others, Cavanagh is critical of how those with power and wealth retain disproportionate influence over government and market outcomes. "Those with money . . . have a wildly disproportionate effect on elections and policies, so the state often exacerbates rather than alleviates the underlying conditions of poverty that cause homelessness—lack of access to healthcare, good education, unionized jobs, treatment for addiction, and so on."[49] Cavanaugh's answer to this, at least in part, is the promotion of subsidiarity. He applies it to homelessness in three ways.

The first way to see subsidiarity at work is through the creation of local institutions and organizations that deal with homelessness. Networks of response emerge from within communities themselves. Cavanaugh describes how some local churches invite the "chaos" of people into their physical spaces, bringing together their church members with those who are experiencing homelessness. This allows churches and faith communities to come face-to-face with the lived reality of homelessness. This clearly speaks to Pope Francis's idea of "encounter," of coming into contact with the suffering of others and allowing ourselves to be changed by it. And it fosters the sort of social proximity that can help dismantle harmful narratives and stereotypes about homeless people.

A second feature of subsidiarity, and one that is arguably more controversial, is Cavanaugh's support of universal basic income (UBI). This is not at odds with the Catholic Social Tradition but does find resistance among some who believe the state has no

[48] Cavanaugh, "Strategies from Below," 150.
[49] Cavanaugh, 150.

business in distributing wealth in this fashion. Cavanaugh argues that this approach could give people the financial freedom to work their way out of homelessness. It is based on the idea that people on the ground know best what they need, but that they need a modicum of assistance in realizing those needs. Cavanaugh says that another benefit would emerge from a UBI approach: it would help dissipate, or at least dilute, the meritocratic ideology that dominates public discourse at present. However, he does raise one note of caution here. He does not want a UBI approach to act as a substitute for human encounter and hospitality. For encountering the fragility, chaos, and brokenness of others forces us to confront these dimensions of our own lives: "This encounter with the fragility of others . . . opens up our own fragility, and that often transforms people into agents building real communal structures of solidarity in the world. I worry that relying on cash transfers could promote a 'culture of indifference' . . . [and] that money could substitute for grace."[50] A UBI approach, therefore, should not become a way of keeping people apart. Vibrant communities depend on subsidiarity and solidarity, and not their "ghettoization." So, although universal basic income could create some of the conditions necessary for the unhoused to become agents of their own change, it must be part of a broader vision of engagement and encounter.

A third way that Cavanaugh applies the principle of subsidiarity happens at the personal level. As care for the poor becomes more institutionalized, we risk depersonalizing and "disincarnating" our response to homelessness. He refers to the Catholic Worker "houses of hospitality" as places into which the stranger is invited. These houses reflect a broader vision where all persons are recognized as children of God, and where the Christian social vision is enacted through hospitality.

For Cavanaugh, responses to homelessness need to "think big" and "think small." Big strategies focus on the root causes of

[50] Cavanaugh, 153.

homelessness, the systemic injustices that exacerbate the problem. As such, these big strategies will require changing sinful structures. But to "think small" moves us toward deeper personal encounter with our unhoused brothers and sisters. It involves building up local networks that will empower individuals and communities, and is centered around the personal encounters that will help dismantle cultures of indifference. To quote Pope Francis, "The Gospel tells us constantly to run the risk of a face-to-face encounter with others, with their physical presence which challenges us, with their pain and their pleas, with their joy which infects us in our close and continuous interaction" (*Evangelii Gaudium* 88).

Conclusion

Given the shortcomings of neoliberalism and its destructive impact on the provision of affordable housing, how do we map a better way forward? It is no surprise that Pope Francis is critical of economic strategies that lead to exclusion, and he questions whether the market can ever sufficiently level the playing field. He lays down the challenge that we each face: we must work together to eliminate the structural causes of poverty and inequality, and work to promote the integral development of all peoples. Moreover, he insists that we must *create a new mindset*, a new way of thinking that emphasizes community and the common good over the appropriation of wealth and goods by the minority (*Fratelli Tutti* 108). For this to happen, we need economic structures that are participatory, democratic, and inclusive. Similarly, in *Caritas in Veritate*, Pope Benedict wrote: "Economic activity cannot solve all social problems through the simple application of commercial logic. This needs to be directed towards the pursuit of the common good, for which the political community in particular must also take responsibility. Therefore, it must be borne in mind that grave imbalances are produced when economic action, conceived merely as an engine for wealth creation, is detached from political action, conceived as a means for pursuing justice through redistribution" (36). And Pope Francis condemns systems and ideologies that place economic priorities ahead of concern for human beings, especially the most vulnerable (*Evangelii Gaudium* 55). We have created structures that exclude, he tells us, and he is critical of the kind of market ideology that allows the powerful to exploit the powerless (*Evangelii Gaudium* 53). Of deep concern to Pope Francis is the throwaway culture that now extends to human beings: "It is no longer simply about exploitation and oppression, but something new. Exclusion ultimately has to do with what it means to be a part of the society in which we live. . . . The excluded are not the 'exploited' but the outcast, the 'leftovers'" (*Evangelii Gaudium* 53).

If the arguments outlined by Bouma-Prediger and Walsh earlier in this chapter are correct, then Catholic Social Teaching provides a framework that allows for a new social vision to be worked out. The idea of the common good provides both the language and vision to push back against the "post-care" society that they describe. And the impact of homelessness is felt far beyond a lack of housing; it makes it more difficult for people to put down roots, integrate into communities, and contribute to the common good. The harm that this causes runs deep. This is why in chapter 4 I turn to the spiritual accompaniment of the unhoused. But next I wish to consider how homelessness can be understood as a denial of human dignity. Chapter 3, therefore, explores the idea of human dignity, and considers how this concept—another cornerstone of Catholic Social Teaching—can assist our debates about the provision of housing.

Chapter THREE

Homelessness as a Denial of Human Dignity

Just Home and Love! the words are small
Four little letters unto each;
And yet you will not find in all
The wide and gracious range of speech
Two more so tenderly complete:
When angels talk in Heaven above,
I'm sure they have no words more sweet
Than Home and Love.

(Robert William Service, "Home and Love")

Introduction

One night, late, I was traveling home on the tram in Boston. It was around midnight, and as far as I could tell I was the only person on the tram. A couple of stops in, a homeless man boarded the tram and sat opposite me. Some young men who got on at the same stop sat a little farther up, and when they spotted the homeless man they moved toward us and began harassing him. It was not physical; it was the macho behavior of young guys trying to show off—strong young men who worked out, wore nice clothes, and were full of confidence. The homeless man ignored them at first but eventually moved up the tram to escape their intimidation. They followed him, and before long he returned, asking politely if he could sit beside me for the remainder of his journey. I said "Sure," but we were soon again joined by the group of men, continuing their intimidation, humiliation, and ridicule.

By now, the homeless man had pulled out a knife for protection, and although I was not afraid of him using it on me, I decided things might escalate quickly. So I confronted the men and told them to move on and to leave us alone. They reluctantly obliged, and my homeless friend thanked me for standing up for him. "This happens every night," he said, "and all I want to do is get home."

I wondered where "home" was for him, and felt bad that encounters of this kind were a common occurrence. Living on the streets was tough enough, I imagined, without the constant anxiety of wondering where the next occasion of harassment, violence, or mockery would come from. As his stop approached he thanked me again; I wished him well, and he went along his way. I too arrived home soon after, somewhat relieved that my journey ended as safely as it had.

This episode can be understood as a failure by those young men to recognize the dignity of the homeless person. At best, they saw him as "an easy target," someone who could be humiliated with little chance of retaliation. At worst, they did not *see* the homeless man at all; that is, they failed to recognize his value as a person. The way they tried to humiliate a quiet, vulnerable person was a violation of his dignity. They wanted to scare him and make him feel as though he did not matter. Insofar as they saw him at all, I concluded, it was in a one-dimensional way; they failed to look beyond the rough sleeper and see the person he was.

This sort of behavior is replicated across society, not only due to an inability to see the suffering of others but also because of an instinct to humiliate that is growing. Think, for example, of the quality of political leadership in some countries, where presidents or presidential candidates resort to ridiculing others as part of their election strategy. The message this sends to society is that humiliation is a legitimate social response. Are we creating cultures where the instinct to humiliate is being nurtured rather than opposed?

The words "human dignity" can easily roll off our tongues. As Christians we proclaim it often, insisting all humans are made in God's image and therefore have an innate dignity. We do not always think about its implications, which are far-reaching. For this is a radically inclusive concept, not limited to those we like, and not lost because of human failure. Christian theology reminds us that although we are all sinners, we possess an innate dignity that must always be defended. The Irish Catholic Bishops' Conference puts it as follows: "Recognising the dignity of all in our society is not an empty formula of words, nor is it mere charitable posture. The Catholic Church teaches that each person, regardless of his or her economic or social position, racial or faith background, must be treated in a manner which fully respects their dignity" ("A Room at the Inn?" 16). The concept of human dignity ought to force us to reconsider our attitudes toward others, and reexamine our social structures and social narratives. And because of this, it compels us to work toward positive social transformation.

The Meaning of Human Dignity

The Christian understanding of human dignity includes certain key characteristics, the first of which is that all humans are made in God's image. This theological statement has a profound equalizing effect, and must translate into the consistent application of this principle. Echoing the late Cardinal Bernardin, Pope Francis speaks of a consistent ethic of life—defending the sanctity is not limited to beginning- or end-of-life matters but concerns the quality of a person's life in its totality. It must include provision for healthcare, respect for bodily integrity, the right to religious freedom, access to decent housing, to name some of the most obvious of its components.

Moreover, Christian anthropology with its Trinitarian underpinnings reminds us that human beings are profoundly relational; we are called to relationship, ultimately with God but also with each other, and we flourish when in right relationship with others. But we are unique, and should enjoy the space to allow what is distinctive in us to blossom. The Irish politician and peace builder John Hume once said that difference is the essence of humanity. By this he meant that no two people are the same, and that difference, uniqueness, is integral to our humanity. Therefore, difference is to be celebrated and not feared—it is a gift and not a threat.

Because we are relational, our affective relations are important for our well-being. The experiences of love, loss, grief, and vulnerability are all part of the human condition. These experiences give content to the idea of human dignity alongside human rights discourse. As Anna Rowlands contends, we must look to these affective relations that shape our lives, to the human experiences of love, loss, friendship, and longing to find the content of what a dignified life is like.[1] This resonates strongly with our discussions about homelessness. Responses to homelessness must of course be concerned with the provision of shelter and broader housing policies. But as I argue in the next chapter, "making spirits whole again" is a crucial part of enacting human dignity. We need, in other words, to enact or establish human dignity through commitment to the spiritual, relational, transcendent, and affective desires of the human person.

A significant moment in both the life of the church and the social doctrine itself occurred during the pontificate of John XXIII, and in the course of the Second Vatican Council, for here we find the full embrace of human rights in magisterial teaching. *Pacem in Terris*, *Gaudium et Spes*, and *Dignitatis Humanae* were arguably

[1] See Rowlands, *Towards a Politics of Communion*, chap. 2.

three of the most significant documents of that era. If we include Pope Paul VI's encyclical *Populorum Progressio*, dealing with the conditions that allow for "integral human development," we find a corpus of teaching that outlines the Christian understanding of human dignity, corresponding rights, and the socioeconomic context in which humans might flourish. Commitment to the dignity of the human person, therefore, is at the heart of Catholic Social Teaching, as the *Compendium of the Social Doctrine of the Church* states: "The whole of the Church's social doctrine, in fact, develops from the principle that affirms the inviolable dignity of the human person" (107).

As we saw in chapter 2, the council fathers described the common good as "the sum total of social conditions which allow people, either as groups or as individuals, to reach their fulfillment more fully and more easily." Importantly, they went on to say:

> There is a growing awareness of the sublime dignity of human persons, who stand above all things and whose rights and duties are universal and inviolable. They ought, therefore, to have ready access to all that is necessary for living a genuinely human life: for example, food, clothing, housing, the right freely to choose their state of life and set up a family, the right to education, work, . . . to proper knowledge . . . and rightful freedom, including freedom of religion. (*Gaudium et Spes* 26)

This is a very positive statement, rooted in a social and interactive understanding of the person. They are not describing the minimal conditions for human survival, but are instead concerned with *human flourishing* and *authentic living*. They imagine the circumstances in which people can live their best lives and achieve excellence. Social, economic, and political structures ought to facilitate human flourishing, protect human dignity, and be *at the service* of the common good, therefore. Housing is crucial of course, for without it other rights and opportunities cannot be realized. As Clemens Sedmak says, acknowledging the dignity of all human beings means "acknowledging the person in her uniqueness, in her mystery, in her special place in creation that cannot be mistaken for a capability-based or a meritocratic or even a civic understanding of dignity."[2] Housing is obviously a critical requirement among the social conditions necessary to live in a dignified way.

The council fathers also named the ways in which human dignity is violated or insulted, including subhuman living conditions, arbitrary detention, deportation, slavery, prostitution, poor working conditions, the commodification of the person and her exploitation for profit, and the selling of women and children. Human dignity is violated in a myriad of ways, and often because of sinful structures in society. In *Sollicitudo Rei Socialis*, Pope John Paul II stated that commitment to the poor and the eradication of structural sins are key to protecting human dignity. And in *Caritas in Veritate*, Pope Benedict named inequality as a threat to human dignity (32). More recently still, Pope Francis identifies the characteristics of what he calls a "politics of indignity" in *Fratelli Tutti*: they include the commodification of the human person, a throwaway culture that now extends to human beings, and a culture of consumerism and consumption that suggests that the value of people is based on their economic contribution to society. As an alternative, Pope Francis asks us to develop a culture of encounter that fosters proximity to the sufferer.

Further Reflections

A very helpful analysis of human dignity is provided by Clemens Sedmak in his book *Enacting Catholic Social Tradition: The Deep Practice of Human Dignity*. Sedmak identifies humiliation as one of the ways in which human dignity is violated. Let us think back to my encounter on the tram in Boston. The homeless

[2] Clemens Sedmak, *Enacting Catholic Social Tradition: The Deep Practice of Human Dignity* (New York: Orbis Books, 2022), 7.

man's dignity was violated by the way those young men harassed and humiliated him. They did not recognize his dignity; they made him feel invisible, worthless, and dehumanized. "People are humiliated when they are 'invisible,' when they are not invited to occupy public spaces. The shaming and shame endured by homeless persons in their experience of not being welcome points to humiliation; persons are humiliated when they have reasons to feel out of place," Sedmak argues.[3] Recognition is one of the ways we uphold human dignity—think of the many people or groups who demand recognition in society. Their invisibility is violating, damaging, and dehumanizing. Failure to recognize another is a form of humiliation.

Honoring human dignity is about a way of perceiving, a way of seeing the world and one another; it is a form of recognition. The encounter on the tram highlights the need to foster the skills to see more clearly, the skills needed to recognize social sin and address structural injustice. The demands of human dignity require that we identify racism, misogyny, prejudice, and systematic discrimination in all their forms, and defend the rights and dignity of those on the margins. In fact, Sedmak goes so far as to say that "blindness to systematic injustice . . . is more than just the indifference of the innocuous bystander. By failing to see, we deny dignity."[4] And what Sedmak says here has implications for everyone's moral journey; for we all must become attuned to the biases or malformed ways of thinking that shape our lives, an essential first step toward moral conversion.

I suggest, therefore, that the concept of human dignity compels us toward positive social change. As a way of seeing, it should inform our concrete practices and make a difference to how we construct society, our workplaces, churches, and communities. Anna Rowlands makes a similar claim, describing human dignity as an *active social principle*, as we will see below. Human

[3] Sedmak, *Enacting Catholic Social Tradition*, 4.
[4] Sedmak, 8.

dignity is a rich concept and needs to be grounded in tangible ways. A potential tension arises between the working out of this concept and its implementation in a specific time, place, and context. Sedmak contends that the Catholic Social Tradition can make a contribution at both ends of this debate—at an intellectual level through its teachings, and practically through its commitment to the poor across the world. Church-based organizations enact human dignity through their work globally with the poor and marginalized. A whole range of church-led projects, aimed at upholding human dignity through the promotion of human agency, freedom, and rights, demonstrates the Christian commitment to justice in the world. For Sedmak, "the enactment of human dignity can follow a script with thick examples in the tradition, a script that tells stories about saints who were committed to a form of life that breathed respect for the dignity of the human person . . . there is a richness [in the tradition] that deepens the loftiness of the concept, paradoxically through the dust and blood of real lives."[5]

Many homeless organizations try to meet the material needs of homeless people, offering food and shelter, and perhaps even some medical services. But some tend to the spiritual needs of the homeless too, providing spaces for prayer and liturgical rituals. The transcendent dimension of the person is sacred, and enacting human dignity also means ensuring that the spiritual and religious needs of people are upheld along with their material needs. I will attend to this point more closely in the next chapter where I include the spiritual dimension of the person in my analysis of integral human development.

Sedmak describes this spiritual dimension of human dignity as its "vertical dimension."[6] The inner and spiritual life of the person is an important feature of human dignity, and deserves care. For this reason, efforts to heal the harms caused by homelessness

[5] Sedmak, 10.
[6] Sedmak, 11.

must respond to deeper human questions of loss, grief, suffering, and vulnerability. The vertical dimension includes the right to religious freedom, for the inner response of the person toward his or her god is an inescapable aspect of human dignity. The right to worship freely, develop one's faith, and strengthen one's relationship with God becomes more difficult in the absence of secure housing, when one is forced to sleep rough or constantly move around. Being part of a church and parish life and being able to contribute to one's faith community is made easier when one can "put down roots." Access to housing plays a critical part, therefore, in protecting the spiritual dignity of people.

Sedmak also identifies the "horizontal dimension" of human dignity. This refers to the social and interpersonal relationships that people form, and how human dignity is expressed and enacted through these relationships. Part of this horizontal dimension is a commitment to solidarity, to recognize others in their fragility and vulnerability. And it implies a willingness to create better societies in which people can be integrated fully and can cultivate the civic virtues that enrich social life.

The third feature of Sedmak's analysis is what he calls the "expressive dimension" of human dignity. This is realized through the exercise of human agency, responsibility, and freedom.[7] Human dignity requires that we see the person as a moral agent, as someone with freedoms and opportunities, and who ought to have a say over the sort of life she leads.[8] But as Sedmak rightly notes, the contributive aspect of social life should not be thought of in a one-dimensional, economics-based way. This is not dissimilar to the way Michael Sandel describes the meaning of work; he sees its economic significance, of course, but emphasizes its cultural importance too.[9] The dignity of the person, in other words, is not

[7] Sedmak, 13.

[8] I would see the capabilities approach of Amartya Sen and Martha Nussbaum as part of this "expressive dimension" of human dignity.

[9] We consider this idea in chapter 4.

confined to their economic contribution. Rather, the expressive dimension of human dignity reflects "a commitment to seeing the being of a person as a foundational, irreducible, and undeniable source of valuable contribution," Sedmak says.[10]

Finally, because human dignity is fragile and can be violated, there is a need to protect it. And so we speak of the rights of persons and the conditions that ensure the realization of those rights. This is called the legal dimension of human dignity, and is seen through the implementation of legal documents, at both the national and the international level. The United Nations Universal Declaration of Human Rights marks a key moment in global efforts to afford fundamental human rights protection under international law.

The Deep Practice of Human Dignity

The four dimensions of human dignity listed above are a helpful way of identifying the concept's deeper implications. Sedmak also speaks of the "deep practice of human dignity,"[11] which includes the task of seeing or recognizing, the task of acting, the task of understanding the person holistically, and the task of protecting the fragility of human dignity. For Sedmak, the deep practice of human dignity is especially important in situations of increased vulnerability and difficulty: "Practicing dignity under adverse circumstances can be called the 'deep practice of human dignity.' It should *not* be exceptional. . . . This is where the imago Dei story is more than a concept; it is a living tradition, an enacted narrative about the human person," he informs us. Another way to explain this is to say that difficult situations form these deep practices. When faced with the uphill challenges of life, those moments that depend on depth of character and courage, people need a deep reservoir of beliefs and values to sustain their efforts. Part of what is also

[10] Sedmak, *Enacting Catholic Social Tradition*, 13.

[11] I borrow this phrase from Sedmak, *Enacting Catholic Social Tradition*.

required here is what Sedmak calls "moral access"—that is, being able to see another as more than a one-dimensional being. "The deep practice of human dignity requires this sense of more (*Magis*), with a sense of the uniqueness and mystery of the person," he says.[12]

For this reason, Sedmak speaks of "dignity literacy." This is a wonderfully rich idea that means the ability, personal capacity, and willingness to see below the surface of people's lives, to have the skills that allow us to look deeper and celebrate the sacredness of all people. This is what was missing in the incident on the tram. But we have to acquire the ability to see the dignity of people, despite the messiness of their lives and the complicated nature of their existence, and to not reduce someone to their present state or to their particular role in life.[13] Dignity literacy is not to be taken for granted—it is something difficult to acquire and easy to lose. We must work at becoming more "literate," more skillful in the art of recognizing and defending human dignity in our world today.

Let me offer a personal example of what I think Sedmak is saying here. My mother had Alzheimer's disease for thirteen years. The condition took hold in stages, and little by little it stripped her of the capacity to do even the most basic tasks, such as feeding herself. Toward the end of her life, she could not speak and had lost all cogitative ability. On one occasion, an occupational therapist came to our home to do an assessment of my mother's care needs. Although Mum could not speak or move, and understood nothing of what was being discussed, this woman spoke directly to her at all times, addressed her by name, and made eye contact with her when speaking about the care that she required. On a practical level the occupation therapist needed to deal with me, for I was making the decisions on behalf of my mother. But at another level, she made sure that my mother was included and recognized at all times throughout that meeting. In other words, my mother was recognized as a human being, with dignity and rights. At no

[12] Sedmak, 22, 28.

[13] Sedmak, 29.

time did this woman speak over her, speak at her, or ignore her presence in the room. It was clear to me that Mum's dignity was being fully respected; she was *seen* as a person with value, dignity, and worth. The fact that this healthcare professional spoke to my mother in the way she did, held her hand, looked directly at her, and engaged with her, made a huge difference to me during what was an emotionally difficult situation.

The way this occupational therapist related to my mother is in contrast to the moral reductionisms that we regularly encounter in society, where people are reduced to single-purpose roles, or perhaps not seen as valuable members of our communities at all. This kind of moral reductionism contradicts the deep practice of human dignity, whereas genuine human encounters make moral reductionism more difficult because we become transformed by the suffering, joy, and lived experiences of others. This is precisely why Pope Francis tells us that we should be "challenged to emerge from our comfortable isolation and to be changed by contact with human suffering" (*Fratelli Tutti* 68).

But of course, this is not always easy. In fact, it might be rather terrifying, or perhaps we are unsure how to best go about the kind of encounter that Francis speaks of. How do we know that we are properly engaging in the deep practice of human dignity? How do we avoid moral reductionism? We need ambassadors, exemplars, to help cultivate a "culture of dignity," especially in the most difficult of times. Perhaps we think of historical figures who stood up and defended the rights of others, often at great cost to themselves. Or we think of people in our own lives who have lit the way by the example they set. In my life, I think of my father and the care he gave my mother as Alzheimer's took hold. He was her principal carer, and for thirteen years he looked after her at home. There were times when things became very difficult, but at no stage did he become angry, resentful, or disillusioned. It must have taken a terrible toll on him, but he saw those years as an act of love for his wife. He remained kind, loving, and gentle throughout it all. His actions were an innate response, emerging instinctively from his love for his wife. Long after my mother lost her ability to speak, long after she lost all recognition of her children, she appeared to hold on to some deep-down connection to Dad, for she always welcomed him with a smile, even in her final days and hours with us. Perhaps her smile was code for a secret world to which only they belonged. My father, without seeking it, became an ambassador for this "culture of dignity," showing his children what it means to love even in the darkest, most painful times.

Human Dignity and Vulnerability

Human dignity is precious precisely because it is fragile. Every day we see how people's dignity is violated. Those of us lucky enough to live in contexts of relative security and freedom may at times fail to appreciate the fragility of human dignity. And yet, human vulnerability is a universal experience; even the most powerful are vulnerable. However, the language of vulnerability is not popular in public discourse, despite this shared human experience. But if vulnerability and human dignity are connected, then the idea of vulnerability could provide us with imaginative access to the plight of those most marginalized in society.

As I mentioned, human dignity can be violated in a myriad of ways. The homeless man on the tram was humiliated; others are objectified; others still are subjected to degrading living or working conditions. In Sedmak's words, these examples "are windows into the concept and into the work the concept can do. There is a link between dignity and vulnerability; in fact, we would not have discourse on human dignity without the experience of vulnerability. . . . In short, the discourse on human dignity is based on the experience of human vulnerability and the exploitation of this vulnerability."[14] I return to the idea of vulnerability in chapter 5, but we can see a link to what Rowlands says about human dignity as "entrusted." Because of our vulnerability we sometimes

[14] Sedmak, 5.

need others to defend our dignity. We entrust it, so to speak, to another for protection. My mother's illness meant that she could not defend her dignity or rights. Her dignity was entrusted to us, her family, to protect on her behalf.

Another theologian writing about human vulnerability is James Keenan, SJ. He explains that vulnerability is part of our nature: "It is the condition for the possibility of our responding, of our being ethical. It precedes our decision, even what we once called the fundamental option," he writes.[15] Our shared vulnerability creates a space of mutual recognition, since vulnerability is integral to our being human and is a common lived experience.[16] It could be argued too that by acknowledging our shared vulnerability we achieve deeper mutual recognition in diverse contexts. This has the potential to lead to a "softening" of social attitudes toward the more marginalized. Could an ethic of vulnerability, therefore, improve the moral fabric of our time? Many scholars believe it could. Bryan Massingale, for example, has explored the connection between solidarity and vulnerability. For Massingale, encounter with and experience of the vulnerable other is crucial to our developing positive ways forward; it is a way to challenge the culture of indifference that contributes to entrenched racism and consumerism. Much like Bouma-Prediger and Walsh, Massingale speaks about how habitus, "incubated through ordinary, everyday practices," can create false consciousness among people: "This habitus creates a barely conscious form of dissonance that inhabits moral responsibility and awareness."[17] Can we say the same about the homeless crisis, and the prejudice that is often directed toward the unhoused? If we are to challenge preconceived ideas about homelessness, surely solidarity, arising from a deeper awareness

[15] James F. Keenan, SJ, "Linking Human Dignity, Vulnerability and Virtue Ethics," *Interdisciplinary Journal for Religion and Transformation in Contemporary Society* 6 (2020): 60.

[16] Keenan, "Linking Human Dignity," 61.

[17] Bryan N. Massingale, "Has the Silence Been Broken? Catholic Theological Ethics and Racial Justice," *Theological Studies* 75, no. 1 (2014): 147.

of our shared vulnerability and precarity, could act as a catalyst for change. To put it differently, can an ethic of vulnerability help avoid the sort of reductionism that Sedmak refers to? I would argue that it can, and would suggest that a richer sense of our collective vulnerability ought to be part of our efforts to counter the consumerist and individualistic ideologies that are dominating public discourse.

Changing social attitudes and creating a new habitus takes time of course, and we are left with the urgent, immediate business of attending to the suffering of those around us. Rowlands, therefore, describes human dignity as something "we are called to help others realize." It is something that we "hold in trust" for others, especially the vulnerable, through the practice of care, she tells us.[18] This resonates with what I discussed in chapter 2 when I considered the connection between care and the common good. If we are in a "post-care" era, as Bouma-Prediger and Walsh claim, then a renewed understanding of human dignity and human vulnerability might help refresh public discourse. For Rowlands, acts of care are not simply acts that are carried out on behalf on another; through acts of care the carer is returned to their own dignity, and "through honouring that of another . . . dignity [therefore] is a persistently motivating, affective driver of human action: the repetition of the idea itself becomes a motivation for moral action."[19]

This is helpful because it allows us to understand the concept of human dignity in a relational, proactive, and dynamic way, rather than thinking of it as static. It is a concept that informs our actions, that moves us out toward others and shapes our activity in the world. In other words, we can say that the concept is an *active social principle*, as Rowlands puts it: "For dignity to be an active social principle requires individuals, groups and institutions who are willing to embody and espouse dignity as a structural practice

[18] Rowlands, *Towards a Politics of Communion*, 55.

[19] Rowlands, 56.

and value. It needs to become both the ritual habit of a particular community and part of its conscious memory."[20] And so, thinking about human dignity as "entrusted" and as an "active social principle" demands that we do more to tackle the injustice of homelessness in our present time. Strengthened by an awareness of our shared vulnerability and precarity, we are accompanied by our unhoused sisters and brothers as we do God's work in this world.

How Human Dignity Is Undermined

Human dignity is undermined in many ways, as we have seen, but Sedmak identifies three general ways in which we disrespect human dignity, each useful for our discussion of homelessness. They are: infantilization, instrumentalization, and humiliation. Infantilization occurs when we treat people as though they are unable to make decisions for themselves or exercise moral agency. It occurs frequently in crisis contexts or with higher vulnerability groups. If we consider the vulnerability of homeless people, we see this dynamic regularly at play. Homeless shelters, for example, provide refuge from rough sleeping and the dangers associated with it. But we know from the testimony of many residents of these shelters that they can be dangerous and disempowering places too. Residents sometimes feel that they are treated like children, with no say over their living conditions and little access to resources or projects that would help build skills. Not every shelter has the space to help with upskilling (woodwork projects, cooking, literacy) or the facilities to allow people to cook their own meals. And there is no doubt that most shelters and hostels are stretched too thin, barely able to cope with demand. But by listening to the experiences of people in these facilities we gain insight into the ways that we (perhaps unintentionally) infantilize them. Sedmak writes, "Respecting a person's dignity requires the effort to give space to the person's agency and decision-making

[20] Rowlands, 56–57.

power, and to avoid patterns of infantilization that undermine a person's self-reliance and self-perception as an (adult) agent."[21] This is a crucial point. Commitment to enacting human dignity and promoting human agency requires us to take seriously the needs of unhoused persons, but this in turn demands that we hear their voice and learn from their experiences.

The second way in which we disrespect the dignity of a person is through their instrumentalization. We see this most obviously through the trafficking of people for the sex industry or the labor market, or through unjust labor practices that devalue the person and limit their rights as workers.

A third way we violate human dignity is through humiliation. "Humiliation is a form of debasing a human person. It challenges the public persona of a person, her reputation, her status; it calls into question the right of a person to be respected," Sedmak says.[22] We humiliate others through our words and actions, when we exclude people, or when we fail to recognize them. Denying people access to adequate, safe housing is an obvious form of humiliation. Being forced to sleep rough, being ridiculed, living in fear on the streets, or having to beg for food further diminishes human dignity. Dignity is also diminished through the humiliation of not being able to wash oneself as often as one might wish, or not having anywhere to relieve oneself. Or think of the "period poverty" that many women experience and the shame that accompanies it. Consider too how more challenging it must be for women and girls who sleep rough; many do not have access to the sanitary products needed to have one's period safely. How must the stress and stigma associated with this add to the deep trauma of homelessness for women, and violate even further their innate dignity?

[21] Clemens Sedmak, *Enacting Integral Human Development* (New York: Orbis Books, 2023), 12ff., 14, 15.

[22] Sedmak, *Enacting Integral Human Development*, 18.

In *Fratelli Tutti* Pope Francis speaks about *a politics of indignity*. By this he refers to the creation of a culture that sees the human person as a commodity, something that can be utilized and discarded. It fosters a culture or habitus that sees human life as disposable and human value aligned with economic productivity. It contributes to the "instinct to humiliate" that I encountered on my tram ride in Boston. For Pope Francis, lasting social change is achieved, therefore, through proximity to suffering, through a willingness to enter into the chaos of others, and through an ability to foster a culture of encounter that can confront damaging ideologies that reduce the person to a commodity.

Enhancing Human Dignity

How, then, can we enhance human dignity? Let us consider the following principles as steps toward uplifting human dignity.

Human Agency

The Catholic moral tradition places great importance on human agency, and its exercise is a feature of personhood. In response to the homeless crisis, some approaches focus on top-down remedies, prioritizing the provision of services or facilities but not always taking account of the insights of homeless people. Homeless charities and street ministries play a critical role in responding to homelessness, often in the absence of government support. But we also must be cognizant of the need to empower people and enhance agency, and not become disproportionately focused on the provision of services. This is something that Laura Stivers mentions in her work, and she is concerned that "we rarely give those who are the recipients of our charity a defining voice in the process."[23] It is important not to miss the opportunity to include the insights of the unhoused in policy-making. There is a

[23] Stivers, *Disrupting Homelessness*, 7.

practical benefit here, since strategies are more likely to respond effectively to local needs when local populations are consulted. But regardless of any tangible benefits that this brings, we can also say that including the voices of unhoused people is good in its own right, because through inclusion, listening, and consultation their agency is strenghtened.

Stivers draws on the work of Traci West, and in particular her idea of "resistance" or "disruptive" ethics, to critique social injustice. West does not speak about disruption for its own sake but rather thinks of it in the pursuit of social inclusion, justice, and equality. Its goal is the creation of communities that can foster spiritual wholeness, participation, and human agency. For Stivers, a Christian response "must also celebrate the agency and spiritual vitality that people exhibit in their embodied responses of resistance in the face of oppression . . . a Christian response to homelessness entails building just and compassionate societies in *solidarity with* the homeless and poor, not *on behalf of* the poor."[24] One interesting model for an agency-enhancing approach is the Finnish "Housing First" initiative. Housing First believes that there should be no "tariff" to entry into a home. It believes: (a) it is a matter of human dignity and social solidarity that we house our neighbor; and (b) it is so much easier to solve problems such as unemployment, mental health, and addiction when one has one's own space and from where one can begin to put one's life back together. This agency-enhancing approach is key to their success, and the Lutheran Church in Finland played a significant part in the implementation of this initiative.[25] Too many approaches are based on an opposing way of thinking—namely, that addiction or mental health issues must be first remedied before someone qualifies for housing. The approach adopted by Housing First should force a rethink of public policy, especially if we believe

[24] Stivers, 8.

[25] See Y Foundation, *A Home of Your Own: Housing First and Ending Homelessness in Finland* (Keuruu, Finland: Otava Book Printing, 2017).

human agency ought to be an essential part of societal responses to homelessness. Erin Brigham also emphasizes the importance of agency for homeless people. Commenting on the Gubbio Project, she says, "More than discovering sanctuary, those who seek sanctuary [at Gubbio] participate in creating it. Sanctuary, in this sense, is marked by a transformation of relationships, where those who have been disempowered and excluded are cocreators of a different experience."[26]

Placing the Voices of the Homeless at the Moral Center

Homelessness is a complex problem, and as we saw in chapter 1, many factors contribute to this crisis. The drivers of homelessness will differ from place to place, and responses need to be intersectional and sophisticated. There may be a temptation to turn to "experts" to solve this problem—whether they be economists, town planners, healthcare providers, government officials, or NGOs. But surely the voices of those at the heart of this problem ought to be heard, and their testimonies used to develop effective strategies. Stivers argues, "The voices of people who are homeless may reflect internalized oppression and should be critically assessed, but clearly a process of empowerment will not occur unless their experiences inform the solutions."[27] An example of what Stivers is referring to here can be found in the Irish experience. For over twenty years, the Irish government has relied on a system called "Direct Provision" centers to house migrants and asylum seekers. Such accommodation is regularly substandard and overcrowded. The centers are run by for-profit organizations and not by the state. Individuals survive on a pittance and have almost every freedom curtailed. Applying for visas and residency is a slow, pedestrian process that has left many people living in Direct Provision for years. One criticism of Direct Provision is that people have nowhere to cook or prepare their own food.

[26] Brigham, *Church as Field Hospital*, 169.
[27] Stivers, *Disrupting Homelessness*, 10.

And especially for women, preparing food for their family is a core part of their identity as mothers and wives. These women feel that their role within the family, as well as their identity and dignity, is being undermined because of these restrictions. Other criticisms relate to a lack of appropriate space for prayer or few educational and play facilities for children. It is a relatively easy thing to fix, and in many cases the people who operate the Direct Provision centers are unaware of the impact these issues have on residents. The experiences, frustrations, and anxiety of residents are rarely heard, but by listening to the people in these facilities, by incorporating their experiences into strategies, by providing a space for people to cook and celebrate their cultural heritage, we honor their dignity and acknowledge their agency as persons.

Responses to homelessness need to reflect the broad, intertwined factors that feed into it. If we value the agency of homeless persons, we ought to listen to the practical challenges they face and consider the ways in which their dignity can be more fully respected. As Stivers explains, "The validity of solutions to homelessness and poverty, must be assessed by whether they actually support liberation in the lives of the people the solutions are meant to help."[28] For this reason Sedmak suggests we "need to move into a second-person perspective, a perspective of encountering the person and 'be with her' rather than (third-person) 'talk about her.' We need to move into the muddiness of experiences if we want to 'enact' the principle, value, and concept of human dignity."[29] Enacting the dignity of our unhoused brothers and sisters, therefore, must include listening to their experiences; it means "being with" rather than "talking at" the unhoused. I turn to this more explicitly in the final chapter when I discuss accompaniment, hospitality, and vulnerability. "Being with" implies building responses that derive from the "muddiness of experience," that are person-orientated, and that cater to the totality of the person.

[28] Stivers, 11.

[29] Sedmak, *Enacting Catholic Social Tradition*, 15.

Identifying Bad Narratives

Damaging social narratives and cultural bias can strengthen oppressive and discriminatory structures in society. We need to ask how our communities—and our churches—allow dehumanizing narratives to persist. It is imperative, therefore, to place the stories of homeless people at the moral center. Because by hearing their stories we not only gain a better understanding of the complexity of homelessness, we also begin to recognize—to *see*—the people at the heart of the problem, which is an important step toward acknowledging their innate dignity. As Stivers puts it:

> In examining the issue of homelessness, the starting point and moral center would not be the experiences of middle-class, white homeowners but the numerous people of low or no income who are without homes and cannot secure affordable rental housing. To get a fuller picture, we would want to listen not only to the stories and struggles of people who are repeatedly on the streets, but also to the stories of individuals and families who are episodically homeless, as well as all the people who scrape by to stay housed and are increasingly losing their homes or rentals to mortgage foreclosure and eviction. Without knowledge of how the experience of each of these groups is different, we will be likely to lump all people who are homeless or poor into one category and label them.[30]

Hopefully this will confront harmful narratives and enact more effective strategies of response. Understanding the specific needs of different cohorts enables us to create better, more strategic responses. The housing needs of single parents, for example, have to be understood in the context of low-paid employment, poor working conditions, and zero-hour contracts. There is also the issue of land value and rising hostility to new developments intended for social or affordable housing. What is sometimes referred to as NIMBYism ("not in my backyard") plays a significant part in

[30] Stivers, *Disrupting Homelessness*, 10.

the current housing crisis. It seems that the instinctive response of property owners is to protect their "investment" at all costs, even if that means blocking housing projects intended for the more vulnerable. This further compounds systemic injustice and denies poorer people the opportunity to secure a home. It is why theologians like Bryan Massingale and Margaret Pfeil speak of complicity in social injustice: "Complicity better captures the (at times) involuntary and inadvertent entanglement with oppression and sinful social structures that arises from a more cultural understanding of [an issue]."[31] Thus, confronting the harmful narratives and unjust stereotypes associated with homeless people is one way we defend their dignity and help compose new narratives that educate rather than divide.

Examining the Dynamics of Power and Privilege

A final point to note is how power and privilege alter our moral agency. It is easy to say that those on the streets had the same freedoms and opportunities as others, and that they are now sleeping rough because of poor decisions and bad life choices. This is, in fact, untrue: not everyone has access to the same privileges, opportunities, or socioeconomic supports, and not everyone exercises the same degree of agency. A meritocratic paradigm ignores how human agency is diminished by unjust power imbalances. It is a paradigm that says we deserve what we have gained, and

[31] Massingale, "Has the Silence Been Broken?," 144. Massingale is speaking here about the social sin of racism and its impact on incarceration rates in the United States. But the point he makes could also be applied to homelessness. If we substitute the word "racism" for "homelessness" we read: "Complicity refers to the ways that whites benefit from, consciously and unconsciously participate in, and contribute to the policies, laws, institutions, and social structures that create, sustain, and perpetuate [homelessness]." For an excellent account of the correlation between racism, white supremacy, and homelessness, see Laura Stivers, "Religious Responses to Homelessness: Addressing White Supremacy and Racism," in *Land of Stark Contrasts: Faith-Based Responses in the United States*, ed. Manuel Mejido Costoya (New York: Fordham University Press, 2021), 140–61.

that those who are poor, homeless, and on the margins are there because of their own failings or poor moral character. This is why some cities have criminalized homelessness, and why police are granted the power to remove unhoused people from lucrative tourist areas. As Stivers notes, "We allow such practices because we can; people who are homeless have little political power."[32] It is worth restating Rowlands's point that dignity is "entrusted," that we have the responsibility to care for, and uphold, the dignity of those who are vulnerable or who are unable to defend their own dignity. Moreover, focusing on the moral failings of homeless people suits those with power and privilege, for it diverts attention away from the root causes of the problem. Importantly, though, Stivers also recognizes that a dualistic approach based on an "oppressor—oppressed" model of relationship is not always helpful. For we all occupy multiple roles and identities, and Stivers explains that although homeless people have less power than others we find multiple roles at play here too, including both oppressor and oppressed.

Churches have a positive role to play in resisting unjust social narratives. For, the job of Christian faith communities is "truth work," as Stivers puts it: "To be involved in truth work today requires a shift in consciousness, moving from a 'consumer/client' notion of citizenship that buys into the commodification of everything (including church affiliation) to a more participatory citizenship that embraces communal resistance and solidarity."[33] She calls for resistance rituals in churches, justice education among the youth, and the creation of spaces for communal sharing of ideas and experiences that can inform church response to social injustice. Stivers believes churches must participate in "strategic conversations" that promote the well-being and dignity of the most vulnerable. This includes strategic listening: "Liberating responses will have to confront inequality and poverty, not simply

[32] Stivers, *Disrupting Homelessness*, 14.
[33] Stivers, 19.

by taking an oppositional stance to dominate culture, but through strategic resistance. . . . Such a movement will not simply address housing policy but will also prophetically address all social and economic policies that create poverty and vast inequality."[34]

Prophetic disruption is about creating compassionate and inclusive societies, as well as creating the spaces for the kind of strategic conversations that Stivers proposes. It requires strategic listening whereby the oppressed take center stage in the conversation, forcing others to become unsettled by their testimony. Churches have a vital, practical role to play here, through their ministries and outreach, and Catholic social doctrine frames that commitment in a corpus of teaching that continues to grow. The church's social teaching captures the deeper meaning of human experience and brings it to bear on a world that is fragile and adrift. As with the Gospel, its teachings are a call to disruption, a challenge to be countercultural and prophetic, to see in each person God's image, and to be willing to always journey to the margins. Living out the Gospel remains an ongoing, unfinished task.

[34] Stivers, 19.

Chapter FOUR

Integral Human Development and Homelessness

What is this room
But the moments that we have lived in it?
When all due has been paid
To gods of wood and stone
And recognition has been made
Of those who'll breathe here when we are gone
Does it not take its worth from us
Who made it because we were here?

(Brendan Kennelly, "We Are Living")

Introduction

These lines, by Irish poet Brendan Kennelly, portray an understanding of "home" that includes more than walls, bricks, and wood. He beautifully captures the essence of what a home should be: it takes its worth from us "because we were here." For many, the idea of home brings to mind a place of security, love, and laughter. When I think of my own home, I think of the people with whom I shared that physical space, including grandparents, siblings, and those who worked for my parents in their business and on their farm. I recall a place that was filled with chat and chant and the telling of stories. I remember the smell of baking as I returned home from school each day—my grandmother's soda bread, scones, and apple tarts freshly out of the oven, waiting to be devoured.

I think of the place where my grandparents died and were waked, remembering vividly the ritual when old men and women gathered to pay their respects, reminiscing on a life now passed, and recalling the adventures of their youth. Home was where my mother died after a thirteen-year battle with Alzheimer's, dying peacefully in her bed and surrounded by her family. And although I have lived in many places as an adult, "home" is still where I go to spend time with my father, the place he has lived his entire life, where his ancestors farmed the land for generations. We sometimes walk the fields together, talking about his animals and the natural world around us. Home was where I first encountered love and encouragement. It was where I witnessed the virtues being lived out daily in ordinary ways by my parents and grandparents, and it was the place from where I was empowered to go out into the world.

But, of course, I have been lucky. For "home" can also be a place of neglect, abuse, and violence, somewhere that is feared rather than cherished. And for others still, home does not exist. For the unhoused, there is no place like home, no place to rest and call their own. As our homeless brothers and sisters struggle to find housing, the happiness, security, and comfort that comes with a home is on hold.

Catholic social doctrine, and more particularly, its teaching on integral human development, tells us that the realization of rights and opportunities is dependent on access to stable, safe housing. Indeed, it is difficult to speak of human flourishing in the absence of a home. And so, commitment to tackle homelessness is a core part of the church's social mission in the world. This chapter will explore the idea of integral human development and its connection with housing, but first let us think about how access to a home can be personally, emotionally, and spiritually transformative.

The Transformative Power of Home

As Kennelly pictures it in "We Are Living," a home is more than a physical building. It can be a place of transformation, and the benefits that come from it extend beyond what the markets say it is worth. Thinking of "home" might conjure up images of the spaces, opportunities, memories, and stories that have shaped and sustained us. Housing security leads to a better quality of life and it can also help increase income levels and allow for better job security.[1] Having a home often instills a sense of pride and enables people to "put down roots." It can foster community spirit and instill a desire to contribute to society. Importantly, it affords a degree of control and agency over our lives. It generates independence, provides surety and security, and helps individuals escape from the precarious existence of having to move from place to place.

Moreover, housing security provides the optimal conditions for the emotional, psychological, and educational development

[1] There is debate about the merits of homeownership versus renting. For some, it may make more financial sense to rent rather than buy a property, and certain geopolitical contexts have a stronger ethos of rental security than others. For example, on continental Europe (in countries like Germany especially) there is a strong culture of renting that differs from countries like Ireland. Renters enjoy housing security because there are sufficient legal checks that ensure that their rights are protected. Moreover, people have the opportunity to secure long-term rental agreements enabling them to remain in a location for a considerable length of time, if desired. By contrast, Ireland's property culture prioritizes homeownership, and rental accommodation is seen as a short-term arrangement. In fact, legal protections for renters are limited, and the rental sector is considered a very unstable and precarious part of the housing landscape in Ireland. The point I am making here, though, is that housing security does not necessarily have to mean *homeownership*.

of children. Children who grow up in a stable environment tend to do better in school compared to homeless children. They are safer, generally, and are less likely to become pregnant as teenagers, and have fewer behavioral problems. One executive director of the housing organization Habitat summed up the importance of homeownership as follows:

> When you bring stabilization to a family, it is not just for this generation but is impacting the next generation. You see kids of families graduate at the top of their class in high school and go on to college. One sponsor [of Habitat] will only sponsor families with young kids because they want to see the difference it makes in children's lives.[2]

A study of the educational needs of children who are homeless or living in temporary accommodation in Ireland reveals the gravity of the situation. Written by Geraldine Scanlon and Grainne McKenna, *Home Works: A Study on the Educational Needs of Children Experiencing Homelessness and Living in Emergency Accommodation* examines how a lack of stable housing is undermining the rights of children in Ireland today.[3] The number of families at risk of homelessness is rising, with detrimental effects for children's development: "In Ireland, families are the largest and fastest growing group experiencing homelessness, and figures from the Homelessness Report from the Department of Housing, Planning and Local Government, February 2018, indicate that children and their families accounted for 63 per cent of Ireland's officially recorded homeless population."[4]

[2] Cited in Stivers, *Disrupting Homelessness*, 91.

[3] Geraldine Scanlon and Grainne McKenna, *Home Works: A Study on the Educational Needs of Children Experiencing Homelessness and Living in Emergency Accommodation* (Dublin: Children's Rights Alliance, 2019), available at www.childrensrights.ie.

[4] Scanlon and McKenna, *Home Works*.

Studies show that children residing in emergency accommodation for long periods have difficulty accessing schools, have poor attendance rates at school, are less able to complete homework on time, have difficulty sustaining relationships with teachers and forming friendships with their peers, experience high levels of anxiety, and typically suffer from poorer mental health.[5] These children also speak about the stigma they feel at being homeless.[6]

On the other hand, housing security can lead to improvements in physical and mental health. Sleeping rough leads to numerous physical and mental health problems. But a better quality of living—that is, not having to rent substandard units or not being forced to sleep rough or rely on hostels and homeless shelters—is enormously beneficial for children's health and development. Typically, they are less stressed and experience less anxiety; breathing-related illnesses such as asthma improve; children's illnesses are easier to manage; access to healthcare facilities such as clinics, hospitals, and doctors becomes less difficult; all of which dramatically improve both individual and family well-being. Adults and children develop a keener sense of belonging to a community. And for children, having a secure home allows them to experience the ordinary things that all children love to do—have friends over on playdates, enjoy birthday parties, wait excitedly for Father Christmas, and go trick-or-treating.

Moreover, there is what one might call a spiritual transformation that comes with housing security; it can help fulfill a person's desire to become part of a church community and become active participants in wider church life. Toward the end of this chapter, I return to these themes when I consider the spiritual accompaniment of homeless people. But what I wish to convey here is that homeownership has benefits that extend beyond economic

[5] Emergency accommodation refers to short-term, temporary accommodation such as hostels, hotels, or shelters. On this point, see Scanlon and McKenna, *Home Works*.

[6] Scanlon and McKenna, *Home Works*.

metrics; there are personal, social, emotional, psychological, and developmental goods in having somewhere to live.

The Meaning of a Home

The Irish Catholic Bishops' Conference issued a pastoral letter on housing in 2018. In it they urge that we stop thinking about housing as a commodity, as an end, and recognize instead that it is a means to a greater human end. Safe, affordable, and appropriate housing is a *human right* and *not* a commodity: "The dignity which, as Catholics, we recognise in every person, must be reflected in the reality of life in our society and it is our belief that safe, affordable and appropriate housing is a human right" ("A Room at the Inn?" 9). The provision of housing cannot be left solely to market forces, and housing policies should reflect the rights of families and aim to achieve greater equality across society. Homelessness, the bishops say, is one of the most destructive consequences of the Irish housing crisis, and they condemn the huge profits being made through speculation in land and housing developments. This has caused tremendous damage across Irish society, and they insist that we must "all work to change this toxic situation; the housing 'market' must serve the people and society rather than further advance the financial interests of a minority" ("A Room at the Inn?" 10, 19).

Critically, the Irish bishops argue that access to adequate housing is fundamental to human well-being, and plays a pivotal role in human flourishing. The right to adequate housing is linked to the realization of many other human rights, such as the right to privacy, freedom of movement, freedom from discrimination, personal security, health, education, and the right to a decent and safe environment. Being able to access educational and healthcare services, being able to enjoy a range of human rights is threatened by the insecurity and unpredictability that homelessness creates. It denies people the opportunity to integrate fully into a community, and to contribute socially, economically, and culturally. What is needed is a new approach to housing that recognizes the deep significance of a home and can challenge the dominant consumerist, market-led worldview of today.

With this in mind, we might turn to a very helpful "phenomenology" of home provided by Stephen Bouma-Prediger and Brian J. Walsh in their book *Beyond Homelessness: Christian Faith in a Culture of Displacement.*[7] In describing the meaning of "home," they underscore what the Irish bishops say in their pastoral letter, and help advance a deeper appreciation of the human connection to place. In total, they offer eight characteristics of home.

First, a home is a place of *permanence.* Nowadays people regularly stay in hotels or Airbnb accommodation, sometimes for lengthy periods of time. And of course people go on holidays, or live abroad when in college or on work placement. There are numerous reasons why people live in various types of accommodation and for differing durations. However, a home implies "spatial permanence." Bouma-Prediger and Walsh say that "in a speed-bound culture, every highly mobile person is a victim of at least some form of homelessness because there is no time to foster a sense of enduring emplacement."[8]

Second, a home is a *dwelling place.* A house, they say, is made of brick, stone, and wood; it is a physical structure. But a home is made from memories, stories, and relationships. This resonates with Kennelly's description cited above: "Does it not take its worth from us / Who made it because we were here?" For Bouma-Prediger and Walsh, a house is a structure devoid of deep meaning, and as such could be thought of as a commodity. A home, on the other hand, is filled with resonance and social significance. And so, "while houses can be bought and sold on the open market, homes can neither be bought nor sold. A home is not a commodity and thus cannot be commodified."[9]

[7] Bouma-Prediger and Walsh, *Beyond Homelessness*, 56ff.
[8] Bouma-Prediger and Walsh, 57.
[9] Bouma-Prediger and Walsh, 57.

Third, a home is a place of *story*. A house becomes a home, they explain, when "it is transformed by memory-shaped meaning, into a place of identity, connectedness, order, and care." As in Kennelly's poem, a home becomes a place of storytelling, song, dance, a place where we inherit an identity through connection with those around us. And there are the rituals that accompany the story-telling, the rituals of participation in homemaking.[10]

Fourth, a home is a safe place of *rest*. It is a place of regeneration and healing. It is where we retreat to, a place of refuge and sanctuary from a frenzied and busy world. Bouma-Prediger and Walsh suggest too that a home can be a place of "enough" in contrast with the consumerist world outside. It is where we cultivate contentment instead of envy, generosity instead of greed, and moderation instead of overconsumption. And when a space becomes a dwelling place of homemaking, "it is not viewed as an anxious achievement, but received as a gift."[11]

Fifth, home is a place of *hospitality*. Rather than a fortress with its thick, high walls, a home acts as a kind of hospice, "a welcoming and caring abode for those—that is, all of us—who are terminally ill." The hospitality of home implies welcome, safety, inclusion, protection.[12] We are received into it, accepted for who we are despite our fragility and failure. In biblical terms, the parable of the Prodigal Son best captures what is meant here. Home is a place to which we can always return, despite everything, knowing that we will be welcomed back.

Sixth, a home is a place of "*embodied inhabitation*." The inhabitants "bear the marks" of their place. Citing the work of David Orr, Bouma-Prediger and Walsh explain that "good inhabitance is an art requiring detailed knowledge of a place, the capacity for observation, and a sense of care and rootedness."[13] We give

[10] Bouma-Prediger and Walsh, 60.
[11] Bouma-Prediger and Walsh, 60.
[12] Bouma-Prediger and Walsh, 60.
[13] Bouma-Prediger and Walsh, 61.

ourselves to a place; we leave our imprint on it, we mold it, and are molded by it too. Describing this as an art suggests that it is something we get better at, perfect, and work on throughout our lives. It is something that develops within us.

Seventh, a home is a place of *orientation*. Or to put it differently, separation from home creates disorientation in our lives. One might recall times of separation—when we move away from home and find ourselves in places new and unfamiliar. Everything feels different, and we long for the familiarity of home, for its smells, routine, and customs. It provides order and orientation; we operate within an order that we understand and have mastered and are comfortable with. Home is the "taken-for-grantedness of everyday practices and discourse."[14] It confers stability, routine, familiarity. There is no place like home!

The eighth characteristic is *affiliation and belonging*. Home is where we find recognition without seeking it; we are among our own, so to speak, and in the space where we belong and can find peace. We are accepted for who we are, feeling whole and complete. And in a theological sense, home is ultimately where we find communion with God.

A similar phenomenology of home is provided by Susan Dunlap. She explains that homelessness is a "problem of embodiment." A home enables us to enjoy a *safe* body, a place where we can escape violence, guns, and attacks.[15] It allows us to enjoy a *clean* body and a *sheltered* body—a place to escape the heat, cold, rain, and snow, and a place where we can cleanse our bodies in privacy; a home gives us a *locatable* body, somewhere we can be contacted, providing an address in order to claim social payments and find employment; a home provides an *eating and drinking body*, where food can be prepared and stored, eliminating reliance on fast food for immediate consumption. It also enables us to cultivate the

[14] Bouma-Prediger and Walsh, 63.

[15] As already mentioned, not every home affords this level of personal security. But Dunlap's point is important nevertheless.

cultural practices of food preparation and sustain important culinary traditions. Home provides a place for a *convalescing body* to rest and regenerate; and it is a place for a *temporal body*, where photographs and keepsakes can be collected and treasured.[16]

What Bouma-Prediger, Walsh, and Dunlap describe is an appreciation of home that has a profoundly rich, deep meaning. It is more than a commodity on the property market—it is something integral to our well-being and our wholeness. It is crucial for the realization of rights and opportunities, as the Irish bishops made clear. But a home anchors us in the world too. Through the stories and rituals of home we forge our identities and achieve a sense of belonging. I do not wish to over-romanticize this notion, however. It is worth restating that the home can be a negative, destructive, and violent space. Nevertheless, if we agree with the features outlined by Dunlap, Bouma-Prediger, and Walsh, we can at least say that the value of a home is broad, rich, and saturated with meaning. Thinking of home in the ways described here also reveals the depth of the interior damage and trauma caused by homelessness. And so, integral human development, which seeks the development of the *whole* person and all peoples, must tend to the internal scars caused by homelessness. We turn next to the idea of integral human development.

What Is Integral Human Development?

Christian anthropology, with its relational, person-focused foundations, promotes an understanding of the person as social, unique, and spiritual. As Christians, we believe that the human being is ultimately destined for union with God, but meanwhile has earthly responsibilities that ought to be honored. When we think of human flourishing, we think naturally of the person's material needs. The social doctrine of the church advances an idea of human development that defends our embodied lives and the material requirements

[16] See Dunlap, *Shelter Theology*, 17–18.

for a dignified life, such as access to housing, food security, water, bodily integrity, income and job security, and healthcare. But integral human development (IHD) is also concerned with the spiritual, emotional, and transcendent dimensions of human existence. There are several features of IHD worth noting at this point.

First, integral human development is closely connected to the Christian idea of human dignity. As Sedmak writes, "Integral Human Development can be presented as an approach that is particularly sensitive to dignity violations and to the ways and forms in which respect for the dignity of persons, especially the most vulnerable persons, are expressed."[17] Additionally, integral human development incorporates understandings of beauty, transcendence, and culture; it includes an understanding of human vulnerability (the capacity to empathize and stand in solidarity with others); it recognizes the importance of imagination and critical thinking; it acknowledges the importance of connection with the natural world, its beauty, and its fragility; and it promotes human agency and defends a person's right to participate in society. Furthermore, IHD occurs where the space to explore the ultimate questions in life exists, and where contexts that foster respectful and meaningful dialogue are cultivated. We might call this the "interior" dimension of integral human development, for it touches those innermost, deeply personal aspects of life, loss, and longing and encourages imaginative thinking. Thus, IHD is a broad, rich idea that requires the social conditions that support its realization. This concept implies a commitment to defend the rights and dignity of the person and to create inclusive, just societies.

For these reasons, Sedmak argues that integral human development "is incompatible with a 'neutral' understanding of development. The concept of IHD qualifies 'development' with a value perspective; it encourages a view that there is no value-neutral development."[18] Social practices reveal values and priorities, they

[17] Sedmak, *Enacting Integral Human Development*, 23.
[18] Sedmak, xxv.

reveal what a people deem worthy of promoting in a particular moment, and they identify who ought to benefit from the fruits of development. Sedmak goes on to say that

> because of the communitarian and personalist undertones, the background theory of IHD is ultimately at odds with the idea of a meritocracy, or utilitarianism and "effective altruism." The common good is a moral good that invites us to see a community as a whole with the imperative of not leaving anyone behind. . . . The idea of integral human development is a common-good-based approach with the aspiration to build flourishing communities on the basis of the flourishing of each of its members.[19]

Although Sedmak believes that IHD forces us to confront the injustices of "underdevelopment," it demands we confront the injustices of "superdevelopment" or overdevelopment too. One might consider, for example, the ecological impact of overdevelopment and ask at what point does development become too much? Citing the work of cultural anthropologist Margaret Mead, Sedmak reveals some of the features of overdevelopment and its fragmenting effect on communities. As early as 1962, Mead warned that the indices of social disintegration in industrial nations included "the indices of crime, delinquency, suicide, divorce, alcoholism, and homicide. These are the current costs of overdevelopment."[20] Today, we see the cost of overdevelopment through these same indices. Scholars like Michael Sandel link rising inequality with "deaths of despair" across the United States, and like Mead, acknowledge the fractures caused by inequality. The human cost of superdevelopment described by Sandel is frightening. The "middle layer" of society is being left behind, he tells us, as is evidenced through greater inequalities in health (both in terms of access to healthcare and in health outcomes) and fewer opportunities for people on low incomes. As a result, many

[19] Sedmak, xxix.
[20] Cited in Sedmak, xxvii.

feel marginalized and experience a deepening sense of despair and disillusionment. Sandel notes how this leads to deaths of despair, most commonly among white adults of middle age. The situation is so bad that today more Americans are dying each year from drug overdoses than died during the Vietnam war. And astonishingly, Sandel reports that more deaths of despair occur every two weeks in the United States than have died during eighteen years of war in Afghanistan and Iraq.[21]

What is happening here cannot be explained by income inequality alone. Inequality is certainly exacerbating feelings of loss, despair, and grief among sections of the population. But grief points to something deeper: people are grieving for a way of life that is gone, they are experiencing nostalgia for the past and are trying to come to terms with the suffering of the present. Economic and social inequality is telling some people that their contribution is worth little and that they are not valued. This message rings even more loudly for low-income workers and those without income who cannot access decent housing or are at risk of homelessness.

By contrast, the concept of integral human development presents a social vision where no one is left behind or discarded. It is an approach that is person-focused and inclusive. Integral human development places at its center the dignity of all people and promotes inclusive social structures. The following sections explore further the socioeconomic implications of integral human development and its significance for homelessness debates.

Economics at the Service of Integral Human Development

In *Populorum Progressio* (1967) Pope Paul VI outlined a vision of development that was inclusive, holistic, and rooted in the

[21] Michael Sandel, *The Tyranny of Merit: What's Become of the Common Good?* (London: Allen Lane, 2020), 200.

Christian understanding of the person. His aim was to explore this concept in a way that took the discussion beyond economic arguments. True development, Paul said, must include economic considerations, but, crucially, it must also take into account the spiritual, social, and cultural dimensions of human flourishing: "Development cannot be limited to mere economic growth. In order to be authentic, it must be complete; integral, that is, it has to promote the good of every man and of the whole man" (*Populorum Progressio* 14). Later, in *Caritas in Veritate*, Pope Benedict wrote: "The theme of development can be identified with the inclusion-in-relation of all individuals and peoples within the one community of the human family, built in solidarity on the basis of the fundamental values of justice and peace" (54). And in *Fratelli Tutti*, Pope Francis echoes his predecessors when he says that "social friendship and universal fraternity necessarily call for an acknowledgement of the worth of every human person, always and everywhere. . . . Every human being has the right to live with dignity and to develop integrally; this fundamental right cannot be denied by any country" (106–7).

The proper goal of development is to build societies where all people can reach their fulfillment, realize their fundamental rights, and live with dignity. Economic prosperity and income security are important, for access to wealth increases our freedoms. But, as Indian economist Amartya Sen explains, "The usefulness of wealth lies in the things it allows us to do—the substantive freedoms it helps us to achieve. . . . An adequate conception of development must go much beyond the accumulation of wealth and the growth of gross national product and other income-related variables. Without ignoring the importance of economic growth, we must look well beyond it."[22] So economic development must be at the service of broader human goals. It must be accompanied by a just distribution of resources, by

[22] Amartya Sen, *Development as Freedom* (Oxford: Oxford University Press, 1999), 14.

the empowerment of peoples, and by opportunities for freedom of self-determination. That is why we speak of integral human development alongside the principles of participation, the universal destination of the world's goods and resources, and a preferential option for the poor. Pope Paul VI was emphatic about the dangers of restricting development discourse solely to economic matters, for this leads to the commodification of the person and to the type of moral reductionism that limits the value of human beings to their economic contribution. Pope Paul insisted that

> all growth is ambivalent. It is essential if man is to develop as a man, but in a way it imprisons man if he considers it the supreme good, and it restricts his vision . . . The exclusive pursuit of possessions thus becomes an obstacle to individual fulfilment and to man's true greatness. Both for nations and for individual men, avarice is the most evident form of moral underdevelopment. (*Populorum Progressio* 9)

Authentic development must be inclusive: it ought to promote the good of the whole person, in her totality, and of all peoples. As Stephen Pope explains, "True development goes hand in hand with expanding networks of solidarity, not exacerbating the gap between the rich and the poor. And it should yield robust intermediate associations, not leave the masses of the poor at the disposal of a domineering few. Its fruits are love and generosity, not greed and arrogance."[23] The Catholic vision of development, therefore, points to something that is not *done* to people; rather, it is about creating the conditions in which individuals and groups can enhance *their own* lives. Integral human development allows people to become "artisans of their own destiny" and "architects of their own development" (*Populorum Progressio* 65 and 76). Thus, human agency is an essential element of integral human development.

[23] Stephen Pope, "Integral Human Development: From Paternalism to Accompaniment," *Theological Studies* 80, no. 1 (2019): 126–27.

The presence of sinful structures inhibit the realization of integral human development. Structures of sin are described in the *Compendium of the Social Doctrine of the Church* as structures that are "rooted in personal sin and, therefore, are always connected to concrete acts of the individuals who commit them, consolidate them and make it difficult to remove them. These are obstacles and conditioning that go well beyond the actions and brief life span of the individual and interfere also in the process of the development of peoples" (119). Thus, at the heart of the social doctrine lies a call to action; as Christians, we bear a responsibility to positively transform the world, to rectify injustice, and to create communities that are more inclusive, equitable, and welcoming. In *Octogesima Adveniens* we read that "it is not enough to recall principles, state intentions, point to crying injustice and utter prophetic denunciations; these words will lack real weight unless they are accompanied for each individual by a livelier awareness of personal responsibility and by effective action" (48). For this reason, Irish sociologist Liam Ryan argued that Paul VI understood liberation as involving positive social and political action *as well as* economic improvement.[24] The liberation of the poor requires more than financial assistance—it must be achieved within, and by, communities empowered to work for their own flourishing. Thus, the principles of subsidiarity and participation operate within the integral human development framework, promoting human agency and recognizing the role that local communities ought to play in their own futures. This point resonates with what we saw in chapter 2, for example, where William Cavanaugh applied subsidiarity to homelessness, arguing that community-based responses play an effective part of broader housing strategy.[25]

[24] Liam Ryan, "The Popes as Modern Social Reformers," *The Furrow* 42 (1991): 98

[25] Cavanagh, "Strategies from Below," 148.

Rejecting Economies of Exclusion

In *Populorum Progressio*, Pope Paul VI warned of the dangers of unlimited capitalism. He described it as "unfortunate" that a system should exist that regards "profit as the key motive for economic progress, competition as the supreme law of economics, and private ownership of the means of production as an absolute right that has no limits and carries no corresponding social obligation" (26). Later popes echoed these concerns. In *Caritas in Veritate*, Pope Benedict explained that economic disparity undermines integral human development: "Through the systemic increase of social inequality, both within a single country and between the populations of different countries . . . not only does social cohesion suffer, thereby placing democracy at risk, but so too does the economy, through the progressive erosion of 'social capital': the network of relationships of trust, dependability, and respect for rules, all of which are indispensable for any form of civil coexistence" (32). He went on to say that the human consequences of economic inequality need careful evaluation, including a deep reflection on the meaning of the economy itself, its goals, and its purpose. Benedict called for far-sighted revision of current economic models of development to correct unjust economic imbalances. This far-sightedness would take into account the damaging effects of rising inequality and the ecological impact of over-development and of economic ideologies based on infinite consumption. Current systems reveal a "cultural and moral crisis" that must be urgently addressed, he said (*Caritas in Veritate* 32).

In the same vein, Pope Francis rejects economies of exclusion, the "new idolatry of money" so prevalent in our world, financial systems that rule rather than serve, and all forms of inequality that spawn violence and division in society (*Evangelii Gaudium* 53ff.). He explains that although some economic policies have enhanced growth generally, they have not promoted authentic human development in a consistent or inclusive way. As a result, "new forms of poverty are emerging," he tells us. And crucially, Francis says, "Poverty must always be understood and gauged in the context of *the actual opportunities* available in each concrete historical period" (*Fratelli Tutti* 21, emphasis added). Moreover, Pope Francis contends that we have become blinded to the inequalities around us; he is mindful of the ways in which sinful structures and cultural privilege deaden our moral sensibilities. He insists that "changing structures without generating new convictions and attitudes will only ensure those same structures will become, sooner or later, corrupt, oppressive and ineffectual" (*Evangelii Gaudium* 189). Francis returns to this point throughout his teachings: what is needed is a reform of unjust structures, but the moral and spiritual crises that underlie them need to be understood also. Francis relies on a virtue-based approach, whereby the human person is called to ongoing moral conversion; people must change their attitudes and generate more authentic ways of relating in addition to reforming social and economic structures.

One of the most devastating effects of inequality is exclusion. Inclusion implies full participation in society, the freedom to contribute socially, and the ability to forge a sense of identity and belonging. Social inclusion takes us beyond mere subsistence; it is about being full and equal members of society, recognized and valued not for what we do but for who we are. Inclusion suggests that we can contribute to the task of creating a social life together and exercise moral agency in our lives.[26] And yet, we continue to see many people being forced to the fringes of society. This is another indication of a "throwaway" culture that is becoming more prevalent today, a culture where humans are dispensable, and their value reduced to their economic output. For these reasons, Pope Francis rejects the "logic" of trickle-down economics, and he queries whether the market can ever sufficiently level the playing field for everyone:

[26] See Kate Ward, "Jesuit and Feminist Hospitality: Pope Francis' Virtue Response to Inequality," *Religions* 8, no. 71 (2017).

> Indeed, "to claim economic freedom while the real conditions bar many people from actual access to it, and while possibilities for employment continue to shrink, is to practice doublespeak." . . . A truly human and fraternal society will be capable of ensuring in an efficient and stable way that each of its members is accompanied at every stage of life. Not only by providing for their basic needs, but by enabling them to give the best of themselves, even though their performance may be less than optimum, their pace slow or their efficiency limited. (*Evangelii Gaudium* 110)

Similarly, William T. Cavanaugh rejects neoliberal arguments that claim that the free market, left to its own devices, will rectify the imbalances in the housing sector. Rebuking those who insist that governments should not allocate goods that the market could otherwise provide, Cavanaugh says that "such voices do not get much credence from those who advocate for the homeless, nor should they. The idea that the market will provide if left alone is one of the most pernicious forms of magical thinking that afflicts the contemporary world, and one that is refuted by the thousands sleeping rough on the streets."[27] I agree with Cavanaugh that our economic structures and policies need to be reassessed in light of a worsening housing crisis. Although effective structural approaches to the housing crisis are needed, people must be willing to alter their mindset too. The significance of housing needs to be understood in a new way, which includes learning from the experiences of those who are unhoused. This is a vital step toward altering the perceptions and stereotypes associated with homelessness. Rather than thinking of homeless people as a threat, or deserving their lot in life, the challenge is to allow ourselves to be transformed by their experiences through authentic encounter and accompaniment. Another challenge is to reevaluate our relationship with housing, learning to see it as an indispensable part of integral human development rather than a market commodity.

[27] Cavanagh, "Strategies from Below," 148.

Finally, there is the challenge of rethinking economic priorities and placing the person at their moral center.

Inequality is not inevitable. Economic policies are human-made and can therefore encompass fairness, justice, and inclusivity should we wish. Inequality is a consequence of bad economic and social policies, damaging narratives that glorify the authority of the markets, and skewed social priorities. Inequality, therefore, can be reduced should society decide to do things differently. Yet, it seems that a major obstacle to integral human development is a widespread apathy and indifference toward the vulnerable. Pope Francis refers to this as the "globalization of indifference." He is concerned that the contemporary world has become immune to the suffering of others and does not hear the cry of the poor, and he believes that a culture of prosperity has deadened us to the needs of the marginalized (*Evangelii Gaudium* 54). He calls for greater solidarity, compassion, and mercy as we face the challenges of living in right relationship with one another.

Inequality undermines integral human development in a host of ways. Many economists too see the need to redress unjust economic structures that have disproportionately enhanced the wealth of the minority. Joseph Stiglitz, for example, has voiced concern about the rising levels of economic inequality in US society. Rather damningly, he says that the American Dream is a myth: "America has not only become the advanced country with the highest level of inequality, but one of those with the least equality of opportunity. . . . We have betrayed one of our most fundamental values. And the result is that we are wasting our most valuable resource, our human resources: millions of those at the bottom are not able to live up to their potential."[28]

Something has gone awry in how we distribute wealth, and wealth is a bad indicator of how society is faring. In fact, as Pope

[28] Joseph Stiglitz, "Inequality in America: A Policy Agenda for a Stronger Future," *Annals of the American Academy of Political and Social Science* 657 (January 2015): 11.

Francis has said, it has now even distorted our understanding of human worth. In his book *The Tyranny of Merit: What's Become of the Common Good*, Michael Sandel examines the commonly held belief that those at the top of society are there on merit. They have earned their place, so the argument goes, while those who have lost out somehow deserve their fate too. Sandel rejects this way of thinking and, like Pope Francis, does not believe that open-market economics alone will solve inequality. Rather than prioritizing greater market freedom, Sandel argues that tackling inequality ought to be governments' fundamental goal: "Mobility can no longer compensate for inequality. Any serious response to the gap between rich and poor must reckon directly with inequalities of power and wealth, rather than rest content with the project of helping people scramble up a ladder whose rungs grow farther and farther apart."[29] The mobility argument—namely, that we are all moving up, albeit at different rates—is misleading. Although we might be mobile, if that mobility is excessively slow, many find themselves falling farther behind despite their best efforts, and making little economic progress in real terms. If inequality continues to widen, mobility alone will not guarantee social and economic improvement. The rungs of the ladder must be adjusted to ensure everyone can progress in a fair, inclusive manner.

Relying exclusively on economic or market-led solutions is dangerous for several reasons, Sandel argues. First, it reduces our understanding of the common good to GDP or other economic indicators. And in so doing, we equate the value of people's contributions in society to the market value of the goods or services they produce.[30] And turning to the market to determine the value of people will risk reducing human beings to commodities. Second, it narrows the civic project and impoverishes public discourse, dominated as it so often is by economic arguments. Third, Sandel

[29] Sandel, *Tyranny of Merit*, 24.

[30] Sandel, 28.

warns that reliance on economic indicators alone reconfigures the terms of social recognition. Deciding who counts and who does not becomes an economic matter rather than a moral one. The dangers of over-relying on the markets are surely obvious: as Pope Francis reminds us: "What is needed is a politics which is far-sighted and capable of a new, integral and interdisciplinary approach to handling the different aspects of the crisis. . . . We cannot expect economics to do this, nor can we allow economics to take over the real power of the state" (*Fratelli Tutti* 177). Francis is hoping to reorient today's dominant narrative, offering a countercultural vision that is highly person centered and relational.

Integral Human Development and Housing

What does IHD mean for homelessness? If adequate housing is placed beyond the reach of low-income workers and those without an income, does this say that only the wealthy deserve access to a home? Is the right to housing a universal right or one to be enjoyed only by the wealthy? Do we need to become more attuned to the marginalization of people within society, as Pope Francis insists, or do we remain indifferent to the suffering and exclusion caused by the free-market economy?

I argued that that economic inequality not only prevents millions from access to a home but is also changing the way we understand its meaning. If we see housing as a commodity, then merit becomes an appropriate measuring tool, and we allow the markets to determine access to this commodity. Seen as a human right, however, affords housing a far deeper moral significance.

Moreover, access to affordable and safe housing is one way of reducing inequality in society. The Irish bishops observed that "housing has become the area where some of the deepest inequality in our society is evident, not just in terms of the housing conditions being experienced, but in terms of the impact of housing expenditure on the level of income available for other needs and on wealth distribution. Allowing a continuing disparity between those who have adequate and affordable housing and those who are poorly housed or without a home will create a more deeply divided society . . . [and] reinforces sharp divisions in society." The bishops say that effectively tackling the housing crisis will not only ensure that individuals and families are housed, but it will also create more equitable, inclusive societies that are vibrant and safe places to live ("A Room at the Inn?" 23). Equitable provision of safe housing is not the only answer, of course, but it is a key part of broader efforts to halt rising inequality.

The Irish context again provides a good example of what I mean here. The bishops have questioned the idea of progress that has dominated much of Irish public discourse in recent years. Without doubt, Ireland has seen considerable economic, social, and cultural improvements over the past thirty years or so. But the bishops rightly wonder whether we can accurately describe this as *authentic* development. There is much inequality in Ireland, and the bishops question whether it is possible to say an authentic development has taken place across society:

> Could we really say that this "authentic development" of the citizen and of our society has taken place if some of the most basic human needs are still unattainable for many of our fellow citizens? Technological innovation, international reputation or the wealth of some, even a majority, does not herald the authentic development of society as a whole, nor is it symptomatic of such. ("A Room at the Inn?" 46)

As I mentioned earlier in this chapter, there are tangible benefits that come with being housed. But there are deeper human goods that arise too, goods that touch the soul and spirit of the person. Lacking access to a home is a denial of the dignity of the human person. In *Sollicitudo Rei Socialis* John Paul II puts this in strong terms when he says that "the lack of housing, an extremely serious problem in itself, should be seen as a sign and summing-up of a whole series of shortcomings: economic, social, cultural or simply human in nature. Given the extent of the problem, we should need little convincing of how far we are from an authentic development of peoples" (17). Housing is a critical building block for enacting integral human development. However, the damage caused by homelessness leaves deep scars, and so the final section of this chapter turns to the interior dimensions of integral human development.

The Interiority of Integral Human Development: Making Spirits Whole Again

Having examined the meaning and significance of "home," I now turn attention to a related question: why enacting integral human development must attend to the spiritual, interior needs of the person. Housing policy, and strategies designed to alleviate homelessness, are largely aimed at the provision of shelter. Some homeless organizations also offer programs that target education, integration, and the upskilling of homeless people. But we must think about the spiritual and psychological damage left by homelessness, and services that focus on healing and reconciliation play a crucial role in enacting IHD.

If integral development is concerned with the totality of the person, then the spiritual, religious, emotional and psychological dimensions of our lives need protecting. This is why, in *Caritas in Veritate*, Pope Benedict XVI explained that integral human development "requires a transcendent vision of the person, it needs God: without him development is either denied or entrusted exclusively to man who falls into the trap of thinking he can bring about his own salvation, and ends up promoting a dehumanizing form of development" (11). The transcendent nature of the person, and one's ongoing journey toward God, must be part of IHD initiatives. M. T. Dávila explains that this "points to the goal of attending to the wholeness of the person, seeing sustained relationship with God and other key elements of personal and communal wholeness."[31] Integral development ought to include creating just and peaceful environments where people can thrive and reach their potential, where they can enrich their faith, and access the spiritual nourishment needed to grow in Christ.

Responding to the needs of our homeless sisters and brothers must include, therefore, tending to the spiritual and emotional harm of broken relationships, unfulfilled hopes, and disrupted promises. And so, making spirits whole again is an essential part of Christ's mandate to love one's neighbor. Homelessness also erodes a person's sense of dignity and worth, and can leave profoundly damaging spiritual and psychological scars. Writing about homeless ministries in the greater Boston area, Dávila says:

> The soul work of homeless ministries—attending to the spiritual needs of the unhoused and the housing insecure—must be part of integral human development. . . . Efforts to address the material needs of the unhoused, of providing adequate shelter, the sense of permanency and routine that are key to feeling safe and thriving as persons and communities, must go hand in hand with attending to the deep spiritual wounds, both personal and systemic, that accompany the precarious life of homelessness and housing insecurity.[32]

Feelings of guilt and shame often shadow the lives of the unhoused. They may experience a profound sense of worthlessness stemming from the regret of failed relationships and unrealized dreams. This is precisely why homeless ministries are so important, for they help people come to terms with their lives and foster healing, forgiveness, and reconciliation. Importantly too, Dávila identifies the role of hope in the lives of the unhoused. Hope comes

[31] Maria Teresa Dávila, "Making Spirits Whole: Homeless Ministries as a Tool for Integral Development," in *Land of Stark Contrasts: Faith-Based Responses to Homelessness in the United States*, ed. Manuel Mejido Costoya (New York: Fordham University Press, 2021), 301.

[32] Dávila, "Making Spirits Whole," 298.

through accompaniment and prayer, through confirming in people the knowledge of God's unconditional love. Rooted in an ethos of accompaniment, these ministries tell people that God's love remains constant, and that God is forever with us, especially in our brokenness and woundedness. Dávila continues: "The soul work of homeless ministries is a key element to bringing wholeness where a combination of life circumstances, choices, and systemic forces has wrought economic and social uncertainty and . . . spiritual harm, resulting in shame and lack of self-worth."[33]

In a similar way, Sedmak speaks of the important role that hope plays in integral human development. A rich inner life emerges through imagination, memories, hope, stories, song, and prayer: "Hope is an important aspect of development efforts, for, in genuine hope, we can experience the power of the imagination and the importance of a sense of what is possible." The importance of "cultivating interiority alongside hope and a sense of the future and alternative worlds" is vital for the enactment of IHD, he says.[34] Although important in its own right, building confidence and giving hope can translate into tangible material improvements. By incorporating hope, imagination and spiritual nourishment, integral development sustains the "intangible infrastructure" of the interior life as well as the tangible infrastructure associated with just, inclusive societies.[35] Recalling Pope Paul VI's definition of integral human development—that it concerns the development of the *whole* person and of all peoples—it is clear that taking "the whole person" into account must include respecting the non-material dimension of life and supporting the intangible infrastructure needed to nourish our interior lives.

An IHD approach also demands a commitment to social injustice and forces us to confront the systemic causes of homelessness. As mentioned above, this includes identifying damaging rhetoric

[33] Dávila, 298–99.

[34] Sedmak, *Enacting Integral Human Development*, 43.

[35] Sedmak, 43.

that labels the homeless as a threat, as disposable, as a drain on society.[36] We are called to counteract deep-seated narratives of shame, working to replace them with a renewed understanding of the sacred worth of all human beings.[37] The neoliberal worldview operates from a narrative that sees the person primarily as a consumer and a producer: one's value is derived from one's usefulness to local and global economic structures. This way of thinking is not interested in how to cultivate meaningful relationships, or in the interior, spiritual nourishment that humans desire. Nor is it interested in creating the conditions that empower people to become active participants in faith communities. But for Dávila, homeless ministries play a vital role in helping individuals reignite their sense of worth and self-belief. She says:

> Spiritually, economic systems grounded on an anthropology of consumption and domination lead to feelings of inadequacy . . . [and shame toward] one's current condition the more removed it is from these destructive measures of being human. . . . The soul work of homeless ministries provides language and imagery to more accurately come to describe one's situation, place one's choices in the scope of systemic forces, and place others' indifference to one's condition in the scope of social sin.[38]

Street ministries provide important spaces for people in other ways too. In addition to providing shelter, some street ministries offer workspaces, places for prayer and contemplation, or quiet spaces where one can get away from the chaos of the outside world. They may provide counseling services or spaces to enjoy reading and listen to music. And *space* is needed to lift up dignity. Housing affords people the space for growth, contemplation, and privacy, all critical elements of well-being. In the chaos of the world, sleeping rough or moving from shelter

[36] On this point see also Dávila, "Making Spirits Whole," 299.

[37] Dávila, 312.

[38] Dávila, 311.

to shelter makes it difficult to find those spaces for imagination, self-care, and retreat. But street ministries can play a role here, and like Dávila, Sedmak believes that integral human development is an approach that honors the "needs of the soul." He describes "beauty, space, rest, and tranquility" as examples of these deep human needs. "Access to beauty and creativity is access to a sense of dignity," he explains.[39] The opposite is true too. Homelessness denies individuals access to the "dignity needs" that Sedmak identifies. Integral human development is about creating the safe spaces for people to come together and forge their identities, feel safe, and foster life-enhancing relationships. It is about providing the spaces where people can encounter poetry, dance, literature, music, and culture, spaces that build self-respect and self-esteem. Homeless ministries foster *resilience* and *resistance* among people, and impart a sense of belonging. This may not lead to any fundamental change of structures, laws, or policies, but there is a different value that we can identify here—the value of recognizing and upholding human dignity. Building resistance and resilience to the scars of homelessness is not easy, but prayer, love, intimacy, and human connection all contribute to our being able to cope in the face of adversity.

Finally, I want to acknowledge the important role of accompaniment in homeless ministry. Taking Pope Francis's idea of a "revolution of tenderness," Mary Scullion and Christopher Williams explain that this revolution is "rooted in relationships and community that, through the power of grace, foster mutual transformation."[40]

Homelessness has become part of the geographical and moral landscape of our time, they say, and it can evoke fear or insecurity in us since it exposes the fragility of human existence. But through accompaniment we come to know the men and women

[39] Sedmak, *Enacting Integral Human Development*, 33.

[40] Mary Scullion, RSM, and Christopher Williams, "Accompanying Each Other on the Journey Home," in Keenan and McGreevey, *Street Homelessness*, 3.

who experience homelessness, and see the distorted way our society values people. Homelessness forces us to confront a fundamental truth, namely that suffering is a universal, inescapable part of human existence and that vulnerability too is part of what it means to be human. But Scullion and Williams believe that by acknowledging human vulnerability we see the dignity of each person in a more profound way.[41] Accompaniment, and the powerful human encounters at its heart, can be both personally and socially transformative. They explain:

> By accompanying those who have suffered through homelessness . . . we discover the grace that empowers us to live more authentically, with mercy and compassion. We experience the power of mutual transformation—and we plant the seeds for a broader social transformation, a revolution of tenderness, a political agenda that is grounded in the Beloved Community that fosters economic, political, and societal structures rooted in the dignity of each person. In doing so, we accompany each other on the journey home.[42]

In the final chapter I look more closely at the idea of accompaniment and how it might enrich debates about homelessness. I argue that the language of accompaniment, hospitality, and vulnerability provide an alternative, richer way of understanding the impact of homelessness. The purpose of this chapter has been to show how the concept of integral human development provides a valuable framework to critique the housing crisis. With its dignity-focused starting point, and its rejection of a consumerist, neoliberalism approach to social issues, we find a vision of development that is built around a holistic understanding of the person. It is a concept that has far-reaching implications, for it requires the cultivation of a new worldview, a new way of seeing our socioeconomic responsibilities, and a new mindset for challenging the dominant

[41] Scullion and Williams, "Accompanying Each Other," 6.
[42] Scullion and Williams, 10.

ideologies of our world. Enacting integral human development will require far-sightedness and courage; it will require adopting the countercultural message of the Gospel and imagining a different world order where the dignity of all persons is prioritized over economic output.

Chapter FIVE

The Art of Encounter, Hospitality, and Accompaniment

Oh, home, let me come home
Home is wherever I'm with you.

(Edward Sharpe and the Magnetic Zeros, "Home")

Introduction

The song "Home" by Edward Sharpe and the Magnetic Zeros tells a story of love and longing. Home here is experienced as a feeling of completeness and contentment that comes with being in love. It points to that secret space shared by lovers, known only to them, accessed often through a smile or touch. The song captures the human longing to be loved, to be in communion with another, and the search for meaning, acceptance, and belonging. Home is certainly a place made from brick and wood, but it is experienced also through the love we encounter and the connectedness of relationship. "Home is wherever I'm with you."

This chapter reflects further on some of the interpersonal and interior dimensions of homelessness. For that reason, the previous chapter, especially what I say about integral human development and spiritual accompaniment of homeless people, is important for what follows.

The Art of Encounter

The idea of encounter is a cornerstone of Pope Francis' theology. But why speak of it as an art? Like any art, it is something we must work at, try to get better at—even perfect. It requires time, effort, and commitment. And the more one practices, the better one becomes. Thus, when we examine concepts like encounter, accompaniment, and hospitality, it is with the understanding that we will not always get it right; but we learn from our failures, thus improving how we relate to those around us.

In her book *Shelter Theology*, Susan Dunlap writes of the presence of horror in the lives of the unhoused. The condition of homelessness is not unlivable, nor is the condition of poverty; many people live with both, sometimes for years. But homelessness and poverty elevate a person's proximity to horror, as she puts it:[1]

> The lived reality of extreme poverty is a world where boundaries of protection, safety, dignity, wholeness, and health are often broken. And once a broken boundary has been experienced once, or five times, or a hundred times, the thought that it may be broken again is always there; in other words, horror hovers. . . . If a wound is a rupture of the body's boundary, skin, then we can also understand poverty as a great wound of the body, mind, and spirit.[2]

Homelessness generates horror in people's lives, causing wounds of the body, mind, and spirit. Even if it is not constant horror, as Dunlap acknowledges, homelessness unmasks dimensions of the vulnerability and fragility that all human beings experience at some point. Homelessness causes a specific type of harm, and the brokenness it creates needs to be acknowledged. Street ministries help the task of healing; they are spaces where the unhoused find shelter, certainly, but also where they can begin reconstructing

[1] Dunlap, *Shelter Theology*, 18.
[2] Dunlap, 19.

their lives. This is an invaluable service and reaffirms the importance of tending to the spiritual and the material requirements of living well. Dunlap writes of the importance of prayer, ritual, and accompaniment in the lives of the unhoused, for through these practices, they find ways of coming to terms with the horror their experience: "Brutal, intractable horror is never far away, but there is respite; there is a witness to the persistence of grace, to a light that cannot be extinguished. We comfort the afflicted, grieve for the ungrievable, and offer each other good news."[3]

This kind of connection contrasts with the culture of individualism that I mentioned in earlier chapters, where we saw how the dominant habitus of neoliberalism leads to cynicism, fear, and a sense of isolation among people. Failure to see "the other" stems in part from social sin and from pervasive cultures that legitimize exclusion. But how do we break from such cultures and begin to relate in a new way? First, we must acknowledge the need for radical disorientation or disruption. Pope Francis locates this process of disruption in the deep encounters we experience with others. It is also important to script a counternarrative, one that recognizes the dignity of all persons, a narrative that acknowledges how social sin and unjust structures contribute to today's housing crisis. Finally, it is important to cultivate a sense of belonging and connection in communities. Kevin Nye contends that homelessness is about more than a lack of housing; it is also about a loss of connection. And when isolation is prolonged, it can have devasting consequences. Isolation causes a deterioration in physical and mental health. For Nye, this crisis of isolation should

> create in us an urgency not only to address homelessness on a grand scale with housing and long-term services, but also to triage and intervene for those who are most isolated, at risk, and languishing on the streets. At the heart of these interventions is the need for authentic human connection. While unhoused people can and do

[3] Dunlap, 27.

> form genuine connections with one another, individuals, churches, and service providers must build the trust and safety that allows for timely introduction of life-saving services and treatments—the types of things a stable social network would typically provide.[4]

Anna Rowlands wonders if contemporary society has lost its sense of fraternity and connection of which Nye speaks. The level of attention to suffering that true fraternity requires can be uncomfortable, since people rarely enjoy acknowledging the reality of vulnerability or fragility. Cultivating a fraternal ethos is not helped by "a culture of well-being," as Rowlands describes it, one whereby people try to avoid upset or being made to feel uncomfortable by the suffering of others. For Rowlands, dialogue and encounter are the basis for a new vision of social fraternity. The "difficult labour" that must be undertaken, Rowlands says, is to "listen, discern, and wait."[5]

The idea of encounter is a cornerstone of Pope Francis's theology. But what do we mean by encounter, and why is it important for our discussions about homelessness? Ilaria Schnyder von Wartensee and Elizabeth Hlabse explore this concept, applying it to integral human development. They identify three characteristics that I think are helpful: first, authentic encounter is always a personal invitation. Second, encounter invites the person to rediscover his or her inherent dignity. Third, rediscovering one's innate dignity enables the person to reimagine a future with hope. In this way, the encounter is "a gaze of mercy." They explain: "Encounter *happens*. It is an unforeseen and unforeseeable transformative event in a person's life."[6]

[4] Kevin Nye, *Grace Can Lead Us Home: A Christian Call to End Homelessness* (Harrisonburg, VA: Herald Press, 2022), 72.

[5] Rowlands, *Towards a Politics of Communion*, 87, 88.

[6] Ilaria Schnyder von Wartensee and Elizabeth Hlabse, "Encounter and Agency: An Account of Grassroots Organization in Uganda," in *Integral Human Development: Catholic Social Teaching and the Capability Approach*, ed. Séverine Denuelin and Clemens Sedmak (Notre Dame, IN: University of Notre Dame Press, 2023), 244.

In the Christian faith we think of encounter in terms of our relationship with God; Christ, in becoming fully human, invites us into genuine encounter, and this personal relationship ought to transform our earthly encounters too. This inseparable link between faith and justice is restated throughout our biblical and theological tradition: commitment to the covenant relationship with God is witnessed through how one responds to the cry of the widow, the orphan, and the poor. As Schnyder von Wartensee and Hlabse put it, "the essential qualities of encounter with Christ become the defining characteristics of one's encounter with neighbors."[7] This inescapably interpersonal dimension is captured by Pope Francis in *Fratelli Tutti* when he says:

> Human beings are so made that they cannot live, develop, and find fulfilment except "in the sincere gift of self to others." Nor can they fully know themselves apart from an encounter with other persons: "I communicate effectively with myself only insofar as I communicate with others." No one can experience the true beauty of life without relating to others without having real faces to love. This is part of the mystery of authentic human experience. (87)

Moreover, Schnyder von Wartensee and Hlabse outline the connection between encounter and agency. Encounter awakens agency when it enables the person to become "the protagonist of her development." Thus, human encounter is understood as an overwhelmingly positive and transformative event in the person's life. Human flourishing is enacted through meaningful encounters that transform how we understand ourselves and others, in turn empowering us to become agents of our own change. Human agency, in other words, can be strengthened through encounter.[8]

This analysis of encounter emphasizes the invitational dimension of right relationship too; we are invited to share in the flourishing of others, but this has to be a free response. Moreover,

[7] Schnyder von Wartensee and Hlabse, "Encounter and Agency," 244–45.
[8] Schnyder von Wartensee and Hlabse, 247.

it emphasizes the interconnectedness of individuals, something captured in the African notion of "ubuntu": this is an idea that reminds us that "I am who I am because of who we all are." Or to put it differently, freedom "implies the responsibility to look after and care for one another, realizing that the other's flourishing is intimately united with one's own," Schnyder von Wartensee and Hlabse explain.[9]

Proximity to the Sufferer

Authentic encounter becomes difficult in a context of widening economic disparity and an ethos of rugged individualism. Susan Dunlap uses the language of "idolatry" to describe how inequality exacerbates social isolation. Idolatry requires a degree of self-deception as well as "the refusal to recognize the depth and breadth of the pain of people of color, the refusal to hear their voices, and the refusal of any suggestion of responsibility for a system of white domination."[10] She identifies white privilege and neoliberalism as two leading factors that result in conditions of extreme poverty in America, exacerbate isolation, and weaken human connection. These idols offer the false promise of escape from the hardships of life; we allow ourselves to believe that these idols will shield us from vulnerability, and so we reject a hard scrutiny of the truth they purport to offer.[11]

Dunlap sees the necessity of resilience in coping with the damaging impact of neoliberalism and white privilege. She describes resilience as the determination to continue living, to keep going, and the inner strength to find ways to survive on the streets in the face of ridicule, anxiety, humiliation, and stress. Recall the encounter with the homeless man on the tram that I described in chapter 3. He had found the resilience necessary to survive

[9] Schnyder von Wartensee and Hlabse, 248.
[10] Dunlap, *Shelter Theology*, 134.
[11] Dunlap, 136.

in the midst of daily ridicule, intimidation, and humiliation. In Dunlap's view, faith can be an important source of resilience: the stories, rituals, and prayers of our religious tradition remind us that God is among us, and they sustain the conviction that every life is valuable, and has an innate dignity. Faith communities help forge connectedness among homeless people, and as Dunlap puts it, "Feeling worth, persistence, hope, agency, and connections is required to emotionally and physically survive living without a home or in extreme poverty."[12]

God's presence is revealed not only when life's problems are solved but also in the dark times, when life's challenges seem insurmountable. God is revealed, in other words, through people's ability to survive *in the midst* of crisis. Dunlap says, therefore, that we need to speak not only of the God who fixes but also of the God who inspires survival, resistance, and resilience: "If the only redemptions that count are climbing out of conditions of precariousness, or advancement towards health and wholeness, or reaching stability, then such transformations are absent for many who live without homes or who live for decades in extreme poverty."[13] Throughout his pontificate, Pope Francis has urged us to go to the poor, to the margins, for God is revealed through their experiences, stories, and suffering. He believes that when we draw near to those on the periphery, establish proximity to the homeless, we draw nearer to God too. Proximity to the margins is a fundamental condition of encounter, therefore, and has been a cornerstone of the Holy Father's teachings.

Proximity to suffering is important for other reasons too, for it is an effective way of breaking social barriers and dismantling unjust stereotypes. It is why Pope Francis calls us to enter into the suffering of others, to get close to their chaos, and to allow ourselves to be transformed by the deep connections that we develop. It is through proximity, openness, and humility that we

[12] Dunlap, 139.
[13] Dunlap, 141.

gain a deep understanding of otherness. And proximity changes both parties—encountering those on the margins reveals to us our own woundedness and our need for redemption and grace. Dunlap speaks of the need to create spaces where this sort of proximity can be realized, where genuine encounter can become more common, and where social transformation can begin: "As more of us engage in the ongoing effort to renounce neoliberal capitalism and white privilege, we will be sustained by the beliefs and practices of people who never had wealth or privilege by virtue of race. The poor are already resisting these powers as the ones who most obviously bear the brunt of them, and we have much to learn." The most important and "sacred" change to happen, she says, is to expand "the universe of people who may be recognized as a friend."[14] Proximity is a crucial part of encounter because it sustains connection, belonging, and relationality—we see others no longer as strangers but as companions.

James Keenan has spoken of Jesuit hospitality as "mission to the marginalized." For Keenan, Jesuit identity is about journeying to the periphery, to those who feel forgotten, ignored, and unloved. He says that the image or model for Jesuit hospitality is the refugee camp because "we are called especially to those who find no dwelling place in this world."[15] The experience of encounter includes a willingness to enter into the chaos of others, a willingness to be proximate, and a willingness to be transformed by what we see.

Proximity of this kind, by its nature, brings us close to suffering. Kevin Nye speaks about the importance of trauma-informed care in responding to homelessness. Trauma-informed care not only recognizes the brokenness of people's lives; it also emphasizes collaboration and empowerment. In understanding the realities that have brought people to their current state in life, we acknowledge the trauma, past and present, that shapes their

[14] Dunlap, 148, 147, 149.

[15] Cited in Kate Ward, "Jesuit and Feminist Hospitality: Pope Francis' Virtue Response to Inequality," *Religions* 8 (2017): 4.

agency. This allows for the creation of responses that are specific, effective, and transformative: "When we recognize the role that trauma plays in shaping people and their behaviour and responses to help, it fundamentally changes the way we see and treat unhoused people. In short, it enables us to love better."[16] The point that Nye makes here is crucial. The quality and character of our encounters matter. True, authentic encounter happens when we meet people where they are at, in all their fragility and failure. And *we* are transformed when we too are encountered, welcomed, despite our failures. As Pope Francis puts it in *Evangelii Gaudium*, "the Gospel tells us constantly to run the risk of a face-to-face encounter with others, with their physical presence which challenges us, with their pain and their pleas, with their joy which infects us in our close and continuous interaction" (88).

Vulnerability

Proximity to suffering forces us to acknowledge our own vulnerability. James Keenan, building on the work of Judith Butler, Enda McDonagh, and Linda Hogan, has written extensively on the connection between vulnerability and morality. He writes, "When we recognize that the word vulnerable does not mean being or having been wounded, but rather means being able to be wounded, then it means being exposed to the other; in this sense vulnerability is the human condition that allows me to encounter, receive, or respond to the other, it allows us to be aware of others and their dignity, to take risks in meeting and recognizing others."[17] Keenan believes that vulnerability is the starting point for our being able to respond morally; it implies a deep awareness of the human condition, which informs how we relate to one another more authentically and strengthen communal bonds.

[16] Nye, *Grace Can Lead Us Home*, 80.

[17] Keenan, "Linking Human Dignity," 59.

I agree with Keenan, and suggest that a deeper recognition of our vulnerability, coupled with a stronger awareness of our interdependence, could help redefine our collective values, and foster greater awareness of social issues such as homelessness. The idea of vulnerability may seem counterintuitive in a political context where power, strength, and decisiveness are considered the prime qualities of leadership. Yet, an ethic of vulnerability might help change *citizens' views* by facilitating recognition of a common human condition, and in turn help create an ethos more open to those on the peripheries. Or as Keenan puts it, "In this mutual recognition we grasp that it is our vulnerability to one another that makes us human."[18] I believe an ethic of vulnerability, together with the idea of care and the common good that we examined in chapter 2, belongs to the foundation needed to generate a new habitus based on connection, mutuality, and inclusivity.

Linda Hogan too argues that awareness of our shared vulnerability can effect positive change at societal and international levels. Applying vulnerability to the international realm, she says:

> Mutual dependence, shared vulnerability, these are elements of human experience that have rarely featured in the ways in which politics is constructed or ethical theories are framed. Indeed, much of our politics and ethics seems to be intent on foreclosing this recognition. And yet shared vulnerability and mutual dependence may be precisely the qualities that have a resonance with the individuals and communities world-wide who are struggling to find the grounds for the hope of a shared future in a world divided.[19]

Thus, an ethic of vulnerability could enrich public discourse and foster mutual recognition among diverse populations, as well as develop a shared vision for public life that is dignity-focused. It

[18] Keenan, 61.

[19] Linda Hogan, "Vulnerability: An Ethic for a Divided World," in *Building Bridges in Sarajevo: The Plenary Papers from CTEWC 2018*, ed. Kristin E. Heyer, James F. Keenan, and Andrea Vicini (New York: Orbis Books, 2019), 219–20.

could also provide a platform of commonality from where we address social injustice and cultivate human connection.

Hospitality

Recognizing our shared vulnerability is a prerequisite of hospitality. In the ancient world, an ethic of hospitality was forged from the harsh, unforgiving landscape of the desert. One had a sacred duty to help the traveler, for without assistance she might not find water, food, or shelter. Tough and rugged surroundings instilled an innate awareness of human vulnerability, precarity, and interdependence among ancient peoples that transcended ethnicity or religion.

Within Bedouin and desert communities, an ethic of hospitality was a core feature of their identity. Hospitality was indicative of a noble character, and a virtuous person was the one who extended welcome to those in need. Thus, Mona Siddiqui describes hospitality as *a way of living*, as "an attitude of simply being with others irrespective of whether they are strangers or friends." It concerns our moral character and involves more than sporadic acts of sharing. And she goes further. This hospitable spirit must push us toward social transformation, forcing us to confront the injustices that put people at risk: "The goal of hospitality as an act and as an attitude to life [has radical implications]; it demands a transformation of the self towards goodness and grace, to how God wants us to be with one another." It involves what she calls the "twin moves of universalizing the neighbor and personalizing the stranger."[20]

This type of encounter, and the hospitality that undergirds it, represents a countercultural worldview to the dominant economic ideologies of today. Rising inequality creates obstacles to authentic

[20] Mona Siddiqui, "Divine Welcome: The Ethics of Hospitality in Islam and Christianity," ABC Religion and Ethics, updated April 3, 2022, https://www.abc.net.au/religion/mona-siddiqui-hospitality-as-welcoming-in-gods-name/12503800.

human development since it strengthens existing social divides and deepens the fractures in society. This is why Pope Francis says that one of the worst effects of inequality is exclusion. Returning to the Bedouin idea of hospitality, and how it was shaped by a dangerous, harsh landscape, one might ask whether we have become disconnected from the moral landscape of our time, a landscape shaped by homelessness and dislocation. Have individualism and consumerism weakened our moral sensibilities to suffering? If so, Pope Francis' plea to journey to the margins, his call for proximity, is crucial for an ethic of hospitality.

Pope Francis believes that we are creating societies that force many to the margins, where they remain forgotten and discarded. And he says this reveals a profound human crisis that drives many social, economic and political injustices. Therefore, tackling injustice will involve the two-fold task of addressing the suffering, despair, grief, and loss that people experience, in addition to finding technical, structural solutions. There is a moral imperative to look inward and find new ways of relating to one another, new ways to foster genuine encounter, and discover opportunities to journey to the margins. For, as I stated above, proximity to the suffering of others can change how we see ourselves, and confirms the need for our own forgiveness and redemption. Kate Ward writes that "the unique word that Pope Francis has to say on inequality is that it's a virtue problem. Not only is it a symptom of certain moral failings in societies, it helps cause moral failings and makes them worse, interfering with the development of virtues like solidarity, compassion, and justice."[21]

Pope Francis condemns the "globalization of indifference" that appears to be taking root in our world and calls for a church that will journey to the margins. He wants a field hospital church where we encounter the chaos of others and allow ourselves to be transformed by that very chaos. Encounter, therefore, must be understood alongside hospitality.

[21] Ward, 3.

But hospitality is a risky virtue, for it involves risk to both the host and the guest: as Ward explains, "Since hospitality by definition is practiced across boundaries of difference, it forces host and guest to acknowledge and embrace their own differences rather than attempting to erase them."[22] However, Ward contends that by offering and accepting hospitality, both host and guest acknowledge their differences and woundedness while nevertheless being willing to encounter each other in a spirit of respect. Difference can generate hostility, of course, and things can go wrong! So, we try to balance the legitimate need for safety alongside the desire to encounter. True hospitality, although risky, ought to be based on mutuality and reciprocity. Or as Christine Pohl says, "The normative practice of hospitality, which in addition to providing food and shelter to strangers also includes recognition, community, and the possibility of transcending social difference, requires hosts who are in some way marginal to prevailing social structures and meanings. Without this marginal dimension, the relation between hosts and guests often serves the more conservative function of reinforcing existing social relations and hierarchies."[23]

There are, of course, limits to hospitality. It is time-consuming and resource-demanding, even for those we like! It can also be emotionally exhausting, and we may need to impose limits for our own good. Moreover, hospitality and the encounter can reveal previously unnoticed biases, laying bare our unjust assumptions.

And hospitality needs boundaries. Boundaries are sometimes thought of in a negative way, as something that sets out spaces of exclusion. And, of course, they can give ideological justification to "our geographies of exclusion," identifying those who count and those who do not. Thick boundaries can become prisons for people rather than places of sanctuary: "Boundaries used to erect fortresses of self-protection, then, can never be refuges of hospitality." But equally, by setting out designated spaces, boundaries

[22] Ward, 5.
[23] Cited in Ward, 7.

become places that we can also invite people into. As Bouma-Prediger and Walsh explain, in the absence of a designated boundary we have nowhere to invite or welcome someone.[24] Christine Pohl makes a similar observation. Hospitality is fundamentally connected to place, "a space bounded by commitments, values, meanings."[25] She goes on to say that boundaries serve an important function since they create a place where we and others can be physically and psychologically safe; they provide a safe, designated space where people who have endured trauma can relax, heal, and find peace. It is for this reason that boundaries often include rules that protect everyone within that space. Hospitality, in other words, is not limitless and might require boundaries that enforce strict rules to protect both host and recipient. One might think of the rules implemented in homeless shelters, rules that are intended not to exclude but to create safe, appropriate spaces for all who reside and work there.

Accompaniment: The Adventure of Hospitality

Why "adventure"? True accompaniment changes both parties, and hospitality, if authentic, should create moments of genuine human encounter rather than reinforce unjust power dynamics. Accompaniment suggests that we are willing to unsettle ourselves, to disrupt our preconceptions. It is the process through which we allow ourselves to be changed by the vulnerable other.

Schnyder von Wartensee and Hlabse helpfully identify a number of characteristics of what accompaniment means. First, they say accompaniment involves reflecting deeply on the meaning of one's life and one's relationships. A second feature of accompaniment is mutuality; as we strengthen our bonds with others, we further enable positive, transformative action. The flourishing of the individual and the flourishing of those around her go hand

[24] Bouma-Prediger and Walsh, 53, 52.
[25] Cited in Ward, "Jesuit and Feminist Hospitality," 8.

in hand. Third, accompaniment is situated in time and place and concerns the person and that unique moment. It relates to the specific needs and aspirations in a given time, and so, accompaniment cannot be defined or evaluated by purely objective, abstract criteria. The focus is always on the person, in her uniqueness and her chaos, and what accompaniment involves will look different according to time and place. Accompaniment always involves deep listening and journeying with the other.[26]

Importantly, genuine accompaniment must also confront the systemic causes of homelessness, most notably poverty, inequality, and violence. It requires dismantling the damaging rhetoric and dehumanizing narratives that describe homeless people as a threat, as disposable, or as a drain on society.

Through accompanying them, we come to know the women and men who experience homelessness; by hearing their stories, we help create a counternarrative to the destructive discourse that bedevils so much public discourse about homelessness. Hearing these stories helps us see the stranger as a person, made in God's image, and it makes real to us the global realities that force people to the streets. That is why I say that accompaniment, and the encounters it fosters, can be both personally and socially transformative, and can help heal the wounds inflicted by the trauma of displacement and dislocation. Erin Brigham agrees that hospitality is marked by mutually transformative relationships. It "offers a prophetic alternative to the idea of private property, particularly the neoliberal view of private property as unlimited, individual, and absolute. It makes concrete Pope Francis' field hospital ecclesiology, which is porous and mobile so it can accompany people in their suffering and meet them where they are at." But neither hospitality nor accompaniment suspend our responsibility to tackle injustice. Finally, it is important to restate that hospitality understood as charity can reinforce the power of the host. Instead, hospitality ought to facilitate the agency of both host

[26] Schnyder von Wartensee and Hlabse, "Encounter and Agency," 249.

and recipient, enabling them "to participate fully in community and fellowship."[27]

Conclusion

For the Christian, the life and ministry of Jesus is characterized by an "ethics of disruption."[28] Christ's ministry is an example of compassion and mercy, but it is also an example of social confrontation. His life tells us that compassion and commitment to social justice go hand in hand. As disciples, we are called to reform the structures, policies, and attitudes that marginalize people, as well as combat damaging narratives that portray the homeless as architects of their own downfall, narratives that compound their shame and stigma, and deepen their feelings of victimization. As Nye puts it, Jesus was committed to "slow relational work—knowing that connection is a healing force that moves us all toward wellness, flourishing, and transformation. The church, at its best, offers the basic human needs of connection and relationship in a world that is increasingly isolated and numbing."[29]

The goal of ending homelessness can appear overwhelming. Homelessness, I have argued throughout this book, is a complicated reality, with many intersecting socioeconomic and cultural problems. It is exacerbated by systemic inequality, racism, oppression, and violence. Eradicating social injustice can seem like a vast, unconquerable chasm to cross, and it may be hard to know where to start at times. For this reason, it is prudent to begin with what is local and immediate, to try to initiate change in our communities and churches. Indeed, local churches are well placed to provide essential services to homeless people, and act as spaces where people find spiritual nourishment and inner healing. They can

[27] Brigham, *Church as Field Hospital*, 170, 171.

[28] For a full account of what an ethic of disruption might look like for homelessness, see Stivers, *Disrupting Homelessness*.

[29] Nye, *Grace Can Lead Us Home*, 80.

become spaces that force us from our comfortable isolation and bring us into encounter with those on the peripheries. And human connection allows us to see the faces, hear the voices, and learn from the stories of our unhoused sisters and brothers. Through encounter, we enter into a deeper communion with homeless persons and with God, a God who became exiled, who was without a home, and who knew the human condition of vulnerability. A God who remains with us in our chaos.

Throughout this book I tried to show the link between homelessness and systemic injustice, and argued that various forms of injustice elevate vulnerability and force people to the margins. Our economic structures have created a habitus, a moral culture, that prioritizes the idols of economic prosperity and privilege over human dignity. Homelessness is but one symptom of a more profound sickness in society, and it lays bare the devastation caused by economic ideologies such as neoliberalism and the fallacy that the markets will solve society's problems. We need political action and civic commitment to tackle homelessness. But we also need to find the spaces for encounter, spaces that form connection with the marginalized, and where, through that encounter, we too can find forgiveness. As Nye says, "This communion resists social norms and upends economic division, enacting jubilee not as charity but as solidarity. When we can foster, come alongside, and join in community with the unhoused, God is glorified, and we are all made more whole."[30] By journeying to the margins, and by encountering the forgotten, we go a small way on the path toward healing our fractured world.

[30] Nye, 103.

Acknowledgments

I wish to express my gratitude to everyone who supported me in the writing of this book. There are too many to mention, but I would like to thank in a particular way those who generously gave up their time to read chapters and offer constructive advice: Pádraig Corkery, Sheena Doyle, Pat Hannon, and Kevin Hargaden. Pat Hannon was also my first teacher of moral theology, and along with the late Vincent MacNamara and Enda McDonagh, instilled in me a love of theology and of teaching. Thank you!

At the Institute for Social Concerns, University of Notre Dame, I am indebted to Connie Mick and Suzanne Shanahan for their encouragement and help throughout this process. And I owe a special word of thanks to Bill Purcell, formerly of the Institute for Social Concerns, who invited me to become part of this Enacting Catholic Social Teaching book series. I am grateful also to the Liturgical Press team who worked so professionally on this production.

Finally, I would like to thank my family who have blessed me with a safe, nurturing home, and who have brought love and laughter into my life. In particular, I wish to acknowledge my parents, Gearoid and Alison, who showed me what the "deep practice" of human dignity looks like through their kindness, gentleness, and compassion.

Bibliography

Abraham, Kochurani. "Resistance: A Liberative Key in Feminist Ethics." In *Feminist Catholic Theological Ethics: Conversations in the World Church*, edited by Linda Hogan and A. E. Orobator, 97–107. New York: Orbis Books, 2014.

Adkins, Matthew. "Homelessness in America: Statistics, Analysis, and Trends." Security.org, June 7, 2024. https://www.security.org/resources/homeless-statistics/.

Annett, Anthony M. *Cathonomics: How Catholic Tradition Can Create a More Just Economy*. Washington, DC: Georgetown University Press, 2022.

Applebaum, Anne. *Twilight of Democracy: The Failure of Politics and the Parting of Friends*. London: Penguin, 2021.

Banks, Mark. "Cultural Work and Contributive Justice." *Journal of Cultural Economy* 16, no. 1 (2003): 47–61.

Beyer, Gerald J. "Strange Bedfellows: Religious Liberty and Neoliberalism." *National Catholic Reporter*, February 15, 2012. https://www.ncronline.org/news/politics/strange-bedfellows-religious-liberty-and-neoliberalism.

Bouma-Prediger, Steven, and Brian J. Walsh. *Beyond Homelessness: Christian Faith in a Culture of Displacement*. Grand Rapids, MI: Eerdmans, 2023.

Boushey, Heather. "How to Make America More Equal." *Finance and Development* (December 2020): 32–35.

Brigham, Erin. *Church as Field Hospital: Toward an Ecclesiology of Sanctuary*. Collegeville, MN: Liturgical Press, 2022.

Camosy, Charles. *Resisting Throwaway Culture: How a Consistent Life Ethic Can Unite a Fractured People.* New York: New City Press, 2019.

Cavanaugh, William T. "Strategies from Below: Subsidiarity and Homelessness." In *Street Homelessness and Catholic Theological Ethics*, edited by James F. Keenan, SJ, and Mark McGreevy, 148–56. New York: Orbis Books, 2019.

Clark, Charles, and Alford, Helen. "The Throwaway Culture in the Economy of Exclusion: Pope Francis and Economists on Waste." *American Journal of Economics and Sociology* 78, no. 4 (2019): 973–1008.

Clark, Meghan. "Modeling a Personal Solidarity in a World of Exclusion." In *Street Homelessness and Catholic Theological Ethics*, edited by James F. Keenan, SJ, and Mark McGreevy, 210–19. New York: Orbis Books, 2019.

Costoya, Manuel Mejido (ed.). *Land of Stark Contrasts: Faith-Based Responses to Homelessness in the United States.* New York: Fordham University Press, 2021.

Crosthwaite, Alejandro. "Youth and LGBT: Homeless, Overlooked, and Undeserved." In *Street Homelessness and Catholic Theological Ethics*, edited by James F. Keenan, SJ, and Mark McGreevy, 79–88. New York: Orbis Books, 2019.

Culhane, Dennis P., and Ann Elizabeth Montgomery. "Homelessness among Military Veterans: The United States as a Recent Case Study in Political Will and Evidence-Based Policymaking." In *Street Homelessness and Catholic Theological Ethics*, edited by James F. Keenan, SJ, and Mark McGreevy, 63–69. New York: Orbis Books, 2019.

Curran, Charles E. *Catholic Social Teaching 1891–Present: A Historical, Theological, and Ethical Analysis.* Washington, DC: Georgetown University Press, 2002.

Curran, Charles, and Richard McCormick (eds.). *Readings in Moral Theology No.5: Official Catholic Social Teaching.* New York: Paulist Press, 1986.

Dávila, Maria Teresa. "Making Spirits Whole: Homeless Ministries as a Tool for Integral Development." In *Land of Stark Contrasts: Faith-*

Based Responses in the United States, edited by Manuel Mejido Costoya, 297–315. New York: Fordham University Press, 2021.

Deneulin, Séverine, and Clemens Sedmak. *Integral Human Development: Catholic Social Teaching and the Capability Approach*. Notre Dame, IN: University of Notre Dame Press, 2023.

Dicastery for the Doctrine of the Faith. Declaration "Dignitas Infinita." Vatican, April 8, 2024. https://press.vatican.va/content/salastampa/en/bollettino/pubblico/2024/04/08/240408c.html.

Dorr, Donal. *Option for the Poor and for the Earth*. New York: Orbis Books, 2016.

Dunlap, Susan J. *Shelter Theology: The Religious Lives of People Without Homes*. Minneapolis: Fortress Press, 2021.

George, Julie, SSpS. "Violence, Violations, and Homeless Women." In *Street Homelessness and Catholic Theological Ethics*, edited by James F. Keenan, SJ, and Mark McGreevy, 43–52. New York: Orbis Books, 2019.

Gomberg, Paul. *How to Make Opportunity Equal: Race and Contributive Justice*. Oxford: Blackwell, 2007.

Himes, Kenneth (ed.). *Modern Catholic Social Teaching: Commentaries and Interpretations*. Washington, DC: Georgetown University Press, 2018.

Hogan, Linda. *Keeping Faith with Human Rights*. Washington, DC: Georgetown University Press, 2015.

Hogan, Linda. "Vulnerability: An Ethic for a Divided World." In *Building Bridges in Sarajevo: The Plenary Papers from CTEWC 2018*, edited by Kristin E. Heyer, James F. Keenan, and Andrea Vicini, 217–20. New York: Orbis Books, 2019.

Hollenbach, David. *The Common Good and Christian Ethics*. Cambridge: Cambridge University Press, 2002.

International Jesuit Network for Development. *The Development of Peoples: Challenges for Today and Tomorrow*. Dublin: The Columba Press, 2007.

Irish Catholic Bishops' Conference. "A Room at the Inn? A Pastoral Letter on Housing and Homelessness." Dublin: Veritas, 2018.

Irish Catholic Bishops' Conference. "The Work of Justice: Pastoral Letter of the Irish Bishops." Dublin: Veritas, 1977.

Keenan, James F. *Moral Wisdom: Lessons and Texts from the Catholic Tradition*. Oxford: Sheed and Ward, 2004.

Keenan, James F. "Linking Human Dignity, Vulnerability and Virtue Ethics." *Interdisciplinary Journal for Religion and Transformation in Contemporary Society* 6 (2020): 56–73.

Keenan, James F. "Vulnerable to Contingency." *Journal of the Society of Christian Ethics* 40, no. 2 (2020): 221–36.

Keenan, James F. "The World at Risk: Vulnerability, Precarity, and Connectedness." *Theological Studies* 81, no. 1 (2020): 132–49.

Lamoureux, Patricia, and Paul J. Wadell. *The Christian Moral Life: Faithful Discipleship for a Global Society*. New York: Orbis Books, 2010.

Massingale, Bryan N. "Has the Silence Been Broken? Catholic Theological Ethics and Racial Justice." *Theological Studies* 75, no. 1 (2014): 133–55.

Massingale, Bryan N. "Conscience Formation and the Challenge of Unconscious Racial Bias." In *Conscience and Catholicism: Rights, Responsibilities, and Institutional Responses*, edited by David DeCosse and Kristin Heyer, 41–49. New York: Orbis Books, 2015.

McCrave, Joseph. "Hospitality." In *Street Homelessness and Catholic Theological Ethics*, edited by James F. Keenan, SJ, and Mark McGreevy, 220–29. New York: Orbis Books, 2019.

McRorie, Christina G. "Moral Reasoning in 'the World.'" *Theological Studies* 82, no. 2 (2021): 213–37.

Mulligan, Suzanne. "Homelessness: Some Theological Reflections." *Studies* 112, no. 448 (Winter 2023): 439–51.

Nye, Kevin. *Grace Can Lead Us Home: A Christian Call to End Homelessness*. Harrisonburg, VA: Herald Press, 2022.

Perkins, Anna. "Moving Again: Women, Catholic Social Teaching, and Disguised Homelessness in Jamaica." In *Street Homelessness and Catholic Theological Ethics*, edited by James F. Keenan, SJ, and Mark McGreevy, 254–64. New York: Orbis Books, 2019.

Pfeil, Margaret R. "Fifty Years after *Populorum Progressio*: Understanding Integral Human Development in Light of Integral Ecology." *Journal of Catholic Social Thought* 15, no. 1 (2018): 5–17.

Pohl, Christine D. "Hospitality from the Edge: The Significance of Marginality in the Practice of Welcome." *Annual of the Society of Christian Ethics* 15 (1995): 121–36.

Pontifical Council for Justice and Peace. *Compendium of the Social Doctrine of the Church.* Washington, DC: USCCB Publishing, 2005.

Pope Benedict XVI. *Deus Caritas Est.* Vatican, December 25, 2005. https://www.vatican.va/content/benedict-xvi/en/encyclicals/documents/hf_ben-xvi_enc_20051225_deus-caritas-est.html.

Pope Benedict XVI. *Caritas in Veritate.* Vatican, June 29, 2009. https://www.vatican.va/content/benedict-xvi/en/encyclicals/documents/hf_ben-xvi_enc_20090629_caritas-in-veritate.html.

Pope Francis. *Evangelii Gaudium.* Vatican, November 24, 2013. https://www.vatican.va/content/francesco/en/apost_exhortations/documents/papa-francesco_esortazione-ap_20131124_evangelii-gaudium.html.

Pope Francis. *Fratelli Tutti.* Vatican, October 3, 2020. https://www.vatican.va/content/francesco/en/encyclicals/documents/papa-francesco_20201003_enciclica-fratelli-tutti.html.

Pope John Paul II. *Sollicitudo Rei Socialis.* Vatican, December 30, 1987. https://www.vatican.va/content/john-paul-ii/en/encyclicals/documents/hf_jp-ii_enc_30121987_sollicitudo-rei-socialis.html.

Pope John Paul II. *Laborem Exercens.* Vatican, September 14, 1981. https://www.vatican.va/content/john-paul-ii/en/encyclicals/documents/hf_jp-ii_enc_14091981_laborem-exercens.html.

Pope John Paul II. *Ecclesia in America.* Vatican, January 22, 1999. https://www.vatican.va/content/john-paul-ii/en/apost_exhortations/documents/hf_jp-ii_exh_22011999_ecclesia-in-america.html.

Pope Paul VI. *Dignitatis Humanae.* Vatican, December 7, 1965. https://www.vatican.va/archive/hist_councils/ii_vatican_council/documents/vat-ii_decl_19651207_dignitatis-humanae_en.html.

Pope Paul VI. *Gaudium et Spes.* December 7, 1965. In *Vatican Council II: Constitutions, Decrees, Declarations; The Basic Sixteen Documents,* edited by Austin Flannery. Collegeville, MN: Liturgical Press, 2014.

Pope Paul VI. *Octogesima Adveniens.* Vatican, May 14, 1971. https://www.vatican.va/content/paul-vi/en/apost_letters/documents/hf_p-vi_apl_19710514_octogesima-adveniens.html.

Pope Paul VI. *Populorum Progressio*. Vatican, March 6, 1967. https://www.vatican.va/content/paul-vi/en/encyclicals/documents/hf_p-vi_enc_26031967_populorum.html.

Pope, Stephen. "Integral Human Development: From Paternalism to Accompaniment." *Theological Studies* 80, no. 1 (2019): 123–47.

Regan, Ethna. *Theology and the Boundary Discourse of Human Rights*. Washington, DC: Georgetown University Press, 2010.

Regan, Ethna. "Human Rights, Human Flourishing, and the Right to Housing." In *Street Homelessness and Catholic Theological Ethics*, edited by James F. Keenan, SJ, and Mark McGreevy, 199–209. New York: Orbis Books, 2019.

Riordan, Patrick. *A Grammar of the Common Good: Speaking of Globalization*. London: Continuum, 2008.

Riordan, Patrick. *Global Ethics and Global Common Goods*. London: Bloomsbury, 2015.

Rowlands, Anna. *Towards a Politics of Communion: Catholic Social Teaching in Dark Times*. London: T&T Clark, 2021.

Ryan, Liam. "The Popes as Modern Social Reformers." *The Furrow* 42 (1991): 42–50.

Sandel, Michael. *Justice: What's the Right Thing to Do?* New York: Farrar, Straus and Giroux, 2009.

Sandel, Michael. *The Tyranny of Merit: What's Become of the Common Good?* London: Allen Lane, 2020.

Sandel, Michael. "What Liberals Get Wrong about Work." *The Atlantic*, September 2, 2020.

Santoro, Carlo. "Friends of the Homeless: Saint John Paul II, Pope Benedict XVI, and Pope Francis." In *Street Homelessness and Catholic Theological Ethics*, edited by James F. Keenan, SJ, and Mark McGreevy, 19–27. New York: Orbis Books, 2019.

Scanlon, Geraldine, and Grainne McKenna. *Home Works: A Study on the Educational Needs of Children Experiencing Homelessness and Living in Emergency Accommodation*. Dublin: Children's Rights Alliance, 2019. Available at https://childrensrights.ie/.

Scullion, Mary, and Christopher Williams. "Accompanying Each Other on the Journey Home." In *Street Homelessness and Catholic*

Theological Ethics, edited by James F. Keenan, SJ, and Mark McGreevy, 3–11. New York: Orbis Books, 2019.

Sedmak, Clemens. *Enacting Catholic Social Tradition: The Deep Practice of Human Dignity*. New York: Orbis Books, 2022.

Sedmak, Clemens. *Enacting Integral Human Development*. New York: Orbis Books, 2023.

Sen, Amartya. *Development as Freedom*. Oxford: Oxford University Press, 1999.

Schnyder von Wartensee, Ilaria, and Elizabeth Hlabse. "Encounter and Agency: An Account of Grassroots Organization in Uganda." In *Integral Human Development: Catholic Social Teaching and the Capability Approach*, edited by Séverine Denuelin and Clemens Sedmak. Notre Dame, IN: University of Notre Dame Press, 2023.

Siddiqui, Mona. "Divine Welcome: The Ethics of Hospitality in Islam and Christianity." ABC Religion and Ethics, updated April 3, 2022. https://www.abc.net.au/religion/mona-siddiqui-hospitality-as-welcoming-in-gods-name/12503800.

Sowle Cahill, Lisa. "Globalization and the Common Good." In *Globalization and Catholic Social Thought: Present Crisis, Future Hope*, edited by John A. Coleman and William F. Ryan, 42–54. New York: Orbis Books, 2005.

Stiglitz, Joseph. "Inequality in America: A Policy Agenda for a Stronger Future." *The Annals of the American Academy of Political and Social Science* 657 (January 2015).

Stivers, Laura. *Disrupting Homelessness: Alternative Christian Approaches*. Minneapolis: Fortress Press, 2011.

Stivers, Laura. "Religious Responses to Homelessness: Addressing White Supremacy and Racism." In *Land of Stark Contrasts: Faith-Based Responses in the United States*, edited by Manuel Mejido Costoya. 140–61. New York: Fordham University Press, 2021.

Thurston, Andrew. "Why Veterans Remain at Greater Risk of Homelessness." *The Brink*, November 9, 2022. https://www.bu.edu/articles/2022/why-veterans-remain-at-greater-risk-of-homelessness/.

Timmermann, Cristian. "Contributive Justice: An Exploration of a Wider Provision of Meaningful Work." *Social Justice Research* 31 (2018): 85–111.

United Nations Refugee Agency. "Refugee Statistics." https://www.unrefugees.org/refugee-facts/statistics/.

United Nations Special Rapporteur on Housing. "Homelessness and Human Rights." https://www.ohchr.org/en/special-procedures/sr-housing/homelessness-and-human-rights.

United States Conference of Catholic Bishops. "Economic Justice for All: Pastoral Letter on Catholic Social Teaching and the U.S. Economy." 1986. https://www.usccb.org/upload/economic_justice_for_all.pdf.

United States Department of Housing and Urban Development. *Veteran Homelessness: A Supplemental Report to the 2009 Annual Homeless Assessment Report to Congress*. December 2010. https://www.huduser.gov/portal/sites/default/files/pdf/2009AHARVeteransReport.pdf.

Vinciguerra, Tebaldo. "Contributive Justice and Ecology: A Contribution after the Encyclicals *Laudato Si'* and *Fratelli Tutti*." *Journal of Catholic Social Thought* 18, no. 2 (2021): 269–81.

Ward, Kate. "Jesuit and Feminist Hospitality: Pope Francis' Virtue Response to Inequality." *Religions* 8, no. 71 (2017).

Ward, Kate. *Wealth, Virtue, and Moral Luck: Christian Ethics in an Age of Inequality*. Washington, DC: Georgetown University Press, 2021.

Ward, Kate, and Kenneth Himes. "Growing Apart: The Rise of Inequality." *Theological Studies* 75, no. 1 (March 2014): 118–32.

West, Traci. *Disruptive Christian Ethics: When Racism and Women's Lives Matter*. Louisville, KY: Westminster John Knox Press, 2006.

World Synod of Catholic Bishops. "Justice in the World." Vatican, 1971. https://www.cctwincities.org/wp-content/uploads/2015/10/Justicia-in-Mundo.pdf.

Wrobleski, Jessica. *The Limits of Hospitality*. Collegeville, MN: Liturgical Press, 2012.

Y Foundation. *A Home of Your Own: Housing First and Ending Homelessness in Finland*. Keuruu, Finland: Otava Book Printing, 2017.